FOOD
GUIDE

SHANGHAI

Angie Eagan
Justina Tulloch
Marybelle Hu

Marshall Cavendish
Editions

PHOTO CREDITS

Victor Wu: pages 32, 33, back cover. Marshall Cavendish International (Asia)
Pte Ltd: page 42 (from *Feast of Flavours from the Chinese Kitchen*);
226 (from *Chef Wan Around The World*)
All other photos by Angie Eagan, Marybelle Hu, Justina Tulloch.

Published by Marshall Cavendish Editions
An imprint of Marshall Cavendish International
1 New Industrial Road, Singapore 536196

Other Marshall Cavendish Offices

Marshall Cavendish Ltd. 119 Wardour Street, London W1F OUW, UK •
Marshall Cavendish Corporation. 99 White Plains Road, Tarrytown NY 10591-
9001, USA • Marshall Cavendish International (Thailand) Co Ltd. 253 Asoke,
12th Flr, Sukhumvit 21 Road, Klongtoey Nua, Wattana, Bangkok 10110,
Thailand • Marshall Cavendish (Malaysia) Sdn Bhd, Times Subang, Lot 46,
Subang Hi-Tech Industrial Park, Batu Tiga, 40000 Shah Alam, Selangor Darul
Ehsan, Malaysia

Marshall Cavendish is a trademark of Times Publishing Limited

**National Library Board Singapore Cataloguing in
Publication Data**

Eagan, Angie.
Shanghai / Angie Eagan, Justina Tulloch and Marybelle Hu. – Singapore :
Marshall Cavendish Editions, c2006.
p. cm. – (Not just a good food guide)
Includes indexes.
ISBN : 981-232-924-2

1. Restaurants – China – Shanghai – Guidebooks. 2. Shanghai (China)
– Guidebooks. I. Tulloch, Justina. II. Hu, Marybelle. III. Title. IV. Series: Not
just a good food guide

TX907.5

647.9551132 — dc21   SLS2005049138

Printed in Malaysia by Times Offset (M) Sdn Bhd

About the Series

For many travellers unacquainted with the intricacies of Asian food, trying the local cuisine in a foreign land is often a daunting task. Add to that the language barrier and many tourists return home with the notion that there is little variety in Asian food or that hotel food is the epitome of what is available.

The series was conceived to help travellers unfamiliar with the local language and cuisine overcome this obstacle. Each book starts out with an overview of the eating habits and customs in that particular city or country. The food of each destination is then presented in a fashion that Westerners can relate to — by food group such as appetisers, salads, rice, noodles, meats and desserts. In some cases, food is categorised by cooking style such as stewed or grilled food. In addition, a short write-up is provided for each local dish, explaining what the most authentic version usually contains.

In many Asian cities, the most authentic and best versions of a dish are often found in some dark, dingy corner of the city that even the locals will find difficult to locate. For safety reasons, the books in the series will focus on outlets that are easily accessible and will not cause visitors to be stranded and fearing for their lives. While most of the outlets recommended by our authors are in the mid-price range, a few on the higher end of the scale have been included to give readers a wider option.

As the world grows smaller, it is inevitable that the foods of other countries, Asian or Western, find a place in the local culinary scene. For this reason, each book will have a section on international foods and where they can be found.

It is our hope that this series will help to open a new world of tastes to all travellers.

All the information contained in this book is correct at the time of printing. However, while some outlets have been around for decades, others may move or fold overnight due to the competitive nature of the food and beverage industry. The authors and publishers apologise for any inconvenience caused but cannot be held accountable if some of the outlets listed are no longer where they should be.

Contents

HOW TO USE THIS GUIDE

Dishes and Restaurants

Outside of China, the standard Chinese menu consists of 30 dishes. However, within China, there are as many combinations of dishes as there are unique geographic regions and local spoken dialects. To give you a full eating adventure, the dishes in this book have been grouped into 11 different categories.

Most of the sections are grouped according to geographic region, which, in a country as vast as China, dictates the ingredients and seasonings available. Religion also influences eating habits in China as tasty vegetarian dishes have been innovated by strict Buddhists for centuries. Similarly, Muslim dietary restrictions have guided food preferences in Xinjiang.

As well as religion, there are also unique ways to eat food such as hotpot style or snacks from street vendors. If you want to experience the real China, these methods can not be missed.

Not Just A Good Food Guide Shanghai is a guide to experiencing the breadth of Chinese cooking while visiting Shanghai. The best dishes from the region are the focal point of each section and the restaurant listings have been grouped according to the type of food that they serve. You will find that most restaurants within a grouping will offer a standard set of dishes, which are the foundation of their regional cuisine. Within this, many also have dishes that are considered to be their speciality.

CHINESE LANGUAGE

For many foreigners, the Chinese language is difficult to master. Therefore, to simplify matters, the name of each dish is written in English as well as *pinyin*. If all else fails, you may take this guide to any of the recommended restaurants and order dishes by simply using the *pinyin* and pointing to the photo of the dish that has caught your eye or excited your taste buds.

Most of the restaurants listed in this guide also have menus in English. Whilst the *pinyin* is consistent, when the Chinese name of the dish is literally translated into English on menus, the English translation can sometimes appear quite entertaining.

There are a multitude of speciality restaurants that can be visited in Shanghai, from those serving snake to dog to animals normally only viewed in zoos. These restaurants are not listed in this guide, although do not be surprised to see a few exotic delicacies popping up for the more adventurous eaters among you.

Understanding a visitor's concern about eating the unfamiliar, the authors have focused on dishes that are considered to be the pride of that region. The ingredients mentioned, therefore, will be those that the average person would be quite comfortable putting on their table at home.

The more adventurous may want to choose one or two exotic dishes from the menu to complement the dishes recommended in this book. If you want to go native, most standard Chinese banquets begin with boiled chicken feet and jellyfish to nibble on as the first round of tea is poured. Another favourite, drunken shrimp are eaten inebriated but alive. They are a good test of your mastery of chopsticks as they have a tendency to jump out of the pot and hop around the table the first five minutes after being served.

Being an international city with a diverse expatriate population, Shanghai serves food from almost every part of the world. To add variety to your eating experience in this exciting city, the book concludes with a list of well-known international restaurants.

The icons used in this book:

Authors' choice picks

Address

District of the city in which the restaurant is located

The closest metro station

Operating hours. Compared to many other major cities in Asia, restaurants in Shanghai are open longer and later, some 24 hours. Times for last orders are negotiable, depending upon your skills of persuasion. Late night snacks and early morning breakfast can be bought from vendors who erect temporary kitchens on street corners and in small stalls. If you know where to go, Shanghai is a city that does not sleep.

V Vegetarian dishes offered. It must be noted that, aside from strictly vegetarian restaurants, Chinese have a loose translation for vegetarian, which does not seem to include fish, shrimp or eggs. If you are strictly vegan, you will need to confirm specifics about dishes as you order them. Little dried shrimp are the standard oversight.

Telephone number. Within Shanghai, there is no need to include the 021 city code. Include it if calling from outside the city or from a mobile phone that does not have a Shanghai SIM card. Most people who initially pick up the phone will not speak English. Unless they hang up on you, wait patiently while they scramble to find the nearest English speaker.

Price range denotes the average amount one person can expect to pay at the restaurant. Most Chinese restaurants are far less expensive than international ones. In most of the local restaurants, a large group can dine like emperors for very little. The local currency is renminbi, also referred to as yuan.

under RMB50

RMB50–100

RMB100–200

RMB200–300

above RMB300

Mode of payment. Not all restaurants in the city accept credit cards and those that do may not accept all cards. Please call in advance to check.

Menus available in English.

HOME DELIVERY

Home delivery service. Shanghai Sherpas offer delivery to offices and homes in Shanghai. The phone number is (021) 6209-6209, website address is http://www.sherpa.com.cn. English speakers answer the phone and take your order. They then enter your phone number into the database and track the destination via this so they will always know where to deliver.

Getting around Shanghai

Aside from walking, the easiest ways to get around Shanghai are by taxi or metro. In this vibrant city, it is easy to hail a taxi at any major street. All taxis in Shanghai start with a RMB10 rate before 11:00pm, which increases to RMB13 after 11:00pm.

A taxi driver should immediately start the meter when you get in the car. In a standard taxi, this would involve folding forward the red 'available' sign in the front window. The meter will then show the starting fare. If the driver tells you that his meter is broken or tries to negotiate with you to ride without the meter, tell him no. If he insists, get out and get into another taxi.

If you are travelling between Shanghai and Pudong, there are certain hours that the main Yan An tunnel is closed to taxis. This is usually during peak weekday hours at the beginning and end of the typical work day. Most taxi drivers will cleverly avoid these restrictions by taking you through one of the secondary tunnels or over one of the many bridges instead.

Some taxis are also not allowed on the motorways. Typically, these are the taxis that look like pickup trucks or small SUVs. It is fine to commission one of these taxis to go short distances, but avoid them if you are going across the city as their inability to drive on the motorway will double or triple your travelling time.

If you are visiting Shanghai and staying in a hotel, you should always carry the hotel's business card with you. A business card is called a *ming pian* and either the front desk or the concierge will happily provide you with one. All taxi drivers will be able to take you back to the hotel if you show them the hotel card. If they are unsure, most carry a mobile phone and can call to ask for directions.

Show the concierge at the hotel the restaurant that you would like to visit before you go out. Have them write down the address in Chinese, along with the closest bisecting streets. If they are unsure, have them call the restaurant to confirm.

For Shanghai residents and those testing their orienteering skills, either the district in which the restaurant is located is listed or the closest metro station. If you suspect that the taxi driver is merrily bluffing and has no idea where the restaurant is, offer to call the restaurant on your mobile and have the person that answers the phone give the taxi driver directions.

The Shanghai metro system has excellent coverage to the downtown area and increasingly better coverage in Pudong and Hongqiao. It is the fastest way to travel between downtown Shanghai and the newly developed area, Pudong. Most of the system is underground, and entrances are well marked at street level. Tell the ticket attendant which district and stop you will be travelling to and she/he will provide you with the appropriate ticket. A ticket will normally cost you from two to four renminbi. The metro lines are marked on the map on page 38.

Tip

Normally, it is easy to get a taxi in Shanghai. However, during rush hour, it can be difficult to find one in Hongqiao or near the Bund. The only other time that taxis become scarce are on extremely hot days, rainy days and public holidays. If you need to hail one, the best strategy is to go to a nearby hotel and wait in the taxi line for one to become available when it drops someone off. Alternatively, take the metro.

The most pleasant way to travel moderate distances within Shanghai is by walking. If you look closely, architectural remnants of the international concessions can be easily detected and Shanghainese are happy to humour you with shortcuts down old lanes and alleyways.

Buses, on the other hand, are often overcrowded and a breeding ground for pickpockets. If you elect to take a bus in Shanghai, keep valuables in a place where they are not easy to get to. Thieves have been known to slash back pockets or bags just to take a wallet.

SHANGHAI
Introduction

Taxi drivers have opinions about politics. Housekeepers have opinions about prices. Office workers have opinions about travel. But the one thing that people from all walks of life in China consistently have opinions about is food. China rates among one of the top food cultures in the world.

For 5,000 years, since the birth of Chinese civilisation, through dynasties, revolutions and regimes, food has been the cornerstone of the culture of China. A meal is the focal point for many events, from family gatherings to reuniting with friends to honouring the noteworthy and sealing a deal.

In no other civilisation has the preparation, preservation, cooking, cultivation and serving of food played such a prominent role as in China. So much importance is given to food that in Chinese kitchens around the world, dedicated gods supervise the task of preparing daily meals.

Food represents goodwill toward others in China. The celebration of national holidays involves sharing food with family and friends and when the graves of deceased relatives are cleaned annually, provisions are left as a tribute. Food is also representative during the mid-autumn festival, where a gift of mooncakes is given to family, friends and business associates. Marriage is celebrated by throwing an elaborate banquet for family and friends, punctuated by cash-filled red envelopes and decorated with multiple costume changes by the bride.

MAKING CONVERSATION

In China, the value of food is deeply embedded in the culture. The polite way of greeting someone is by asking, "Have you eaten yet?". If you want to move small talk to something more in-depth, raise the topic of food with a Chinese person. Ask them their favourite regional cuisine, their favourite dish, who prepares the food in the family, their favourite restaurants ... and all of a sudden you have a detailed, lively conversation full of passion and viewpoints.

Food is eaten with intent in China. The Chinese believe that the body is made up of an energy force called qi, and that if your qi is off balance it can be corrected with the type of food that you eat. Certain symptoms mean that your body is too hot, and so you must eat cold food like bitter melon, cucumber and celery. During the winter, you need to balance the effects of the weather on your body by eating hot food like mango, orange and hot green chilli.

Chinese are connoisseurs of taste and spend a great deal of time analysing a meal. It is typical for comment to be made upon the freshness of ingredients, the subtlety of a particular underlying flavour and the skill of the chef.

While home cooking is valued, entire families meet regularly at their favourite restaurants to enjoy dishes that

are house specialities. For example, people have been known to meet often at a hole-in-the-wall, two-storey noodle house in Hongqiao specifically to eat the seafood noodles. Similarly, one man religiously worships the hairy crab dumplings in a small restaurant situated a five-minute walk from his house. One of the joys of living in Shanghai is finding your local favourites while

Consistent throughout China in the preparation of food is the use of pork, poultry, seafood and fresh vegetables. The only variation to this is Xinjiang, where religious beliefs have made mutton a mainstay in cooking.

at the same time sampling the continual flow of new restaurants that distinguish Shanghai as one of the best new places to eat in the world.

Not Just A Good Food Guide Shanghai focuses primarily on the food available in Shanghai from six geographically unique regions of greater China: Shanghai and the cities that share its waterways, Beijing and the temperate north, Canton in the south, Sichuan and its spicy cousins, Muslim-influenced Xinjiang and the island of Taiwan.

However, it is fitting that a guide on eating in Shanghai should not only include dishes from all parts of China, but also internationally. Shanghai is, after all, a city born from the interest of the rest of the world. This vibrant city originated as

a small fishing village at about the same time Australia and the United States became nations. It attracted people from around the world and other parts of China who wished to trade and do business. At the turn of the century, Shanghai was one of the main trading ports in the world.

Such an historic role has influenced the cuisine now found in Shanghai. The food style in this bustling city has evolved over time, inspired by the tastes and influences of those emigrating to it from other regions in China. One of the driving influences in Shanghai food is the availability of fresh ingredients on the Yangtze River Delta. Fresh seafood, produce, Shaoxing wines from nearby Zhejiang and rice and tea leaves from the fields above Hangzhou were all important ingredients that have driven the character and style of Shanghainese cooking.

Regional cooking differences

While Shanghai cooking employs steaming, dishes from north China are usually braised or stir-fried. Ingredients in dishes prepared in north China are typically meat and root vegetables and no northern meal is complete without noodles or dumplings.

Xinjiang food is influenced by its age-old ties to the Middle East, as an ancient outpost of the Silk Road. The food in this region is typically hearty and filling with bread, meat, rice and root vegetables frequently featured. It makes use of unusual spices such as cumin, that are unique in Chinese cuisine.

Cantonese food is argued by some to be the most refined in China. Fresh ingredients and a tradition of small snacks, known as dim sum, have made Cantonese food famous worldwide. Much of what is now known as Chinese food in other parts of the world originated in Guangdong province.

Western cooking, exemplified by the Sichuan region, is heavy-handed with mouth shattering red hot spices. The experience can be attributed to a liberal use of red chillies in every form — pickled chillies, chilli oil, dried chillies etc.

Benefitting from its location in the South China Sea, the island of Taiwan offers cuisine which includes an abundant choice of seafood. Being a semi-tropical region, Taiwan sells many fresh fruit

shaved ices and smoothies, which are indulged in by those who have a sweet tooth.

Shanghai has crabs

The uninitiated may be baffled by the signs that are visible at Shanghai's domestic airport every autumn. Each check-in counter displays a picture of a crab, wound tightly with string. The picture has a red cross running through it to denote that hairy crab can not be checked in. This rule has been passed down after years of circus-like exploits where a box breaks or bag opens and a check-in counter erupts in a frenzy of frantically escaping live crabs.

One of the few things that most Chinese will agree upon when it comes to food is that the hairy crab is unequaled as a delicacy. People from across China and parts of Asia schedule their travel to Shanghai to coincide with hairy crab season. Eaten with tender ginger and dipped in red vinegar, Shanghai hairy crab is a unique regional delicacy that is a must for any Shanghai eating adventure.

Eating on the run

Shanghai is a city on the move. It emits a vibrating hum 24 hours a day as deals are done, fortunes made and opportunities lost. Each morning, 15 million people get out of bed, determined to make their mark on the world and many of those 15 million begin their day by eating breakfast on the run.

Typically, their morning begins with a quick stop at a street side stall en route to work. Here, they will pick up a vegetable bun, a meat dumpling or a steaming cup of soya milk and a long doughnut stick to dip into it. The same stalls also serve lunchtime noodles and will provide a small stool so customers can sit and quickly slurp down a bowl of noodles. The meal will end with a grand finale of tipping back the bowl and shovelling the last juice and noodle remnants into the mouth. So interesting is the Shanghai style of eating on the run that an entire section of this book has been dedicated to explaining it. To truly experience the life of a Shanghainese, even temporarily, one must experience eating on the run Shanghai-style.

The art of tea

Tea has played a vital role in China throughout recorded history. It is an industry which generates jobs, has distinguished scholars, has been used as currency and cash, and is an important component of any meal or meeting. Through its gentle fragrant steam, many important decisions have been made in China. Whether between Mao and Nixon or husband and wife, a cup of tea was and is always within reach.

Although there are thousands of varieties of tea grown in China, there are three main types which stand out: green, red and black. One of the most famous teas in China comes from near Shanghai, a place called Dragon Well that sits in the hills

TEA HOUSES

Every district in Shanghai has a number of tea houses. Here, students review lessons, friends play cards, lovers chat and rivals spar. Some of the older tea houses in the city are also used as venues in which local celebrities perform 'double-speak', a form of comedy where the entertainer uses the double meaning of words in Chinese to poke fun at others and life.

above the city of Hanghzhou. It is possible to visit Dragon Well on a day trip from Shanghai and a hike in its tea fields is a journey close to the heart of the ancient spirit of China. Visitors can stop en route and watch farmers slowly swirl the tender young tea shoots around the rim of a hot steel vat, a ritual that produces the famous Longjian tea that has made Dragon Well world-famous.

Knowing about jiu

The Chinese expression *jiu* means alcohol. *Bai jiu* is a potent grain-based liquor, *pi jiu* is beer and *hong jiu* is red wine. Ingredients used in Chinese alcoholic beverages are varied, although sorghum-based *mao tai*, hop-based beers and grape- and rice-based wines are the most commonly consumed.

Chinese people have a strong tradition of drinking alcohol. Most drinking is done while eating at banquets, as it is against Chinese tradition to drink on an empty stomach.

One of the most famous rice wines, called Shaoxing wine, is from Zhejiang Province which neighbours Shanghai to the south. In addition to being a favourite drinking wine, Shaoxing wine is a common ingredient used to cook food in the regions of eastern China.

All of the Chinese restaurants listed in this guide will offer a variety of *jiu*, some as familiar as Qingdao beer and others as unique as Shaoxing wine. *Jiu* is to Chinese dining as wine is to eating in France or Italy.

Dining practicalities

Finding a seat

The average Chinese restaurant does not take a reservation for a small group. There will normally be a person at the door who keeps track of available tables and directs waiting groups to them. Chinese dislike waiting in line and are notorious for working their way up the queue if an opportunity presents itself. Therefore, to get seated in a busy restaurant, you will need to carefully track and defend your position. You may even need to keep an eye out for an available table and when it is your turn, claim it by sitting down as it is being cleared.

When booking for a group of eight or more, restaurants normally have private rooms that will be made available to you if you promise to spend a minimum amount on food. These rooms come with their own waiters and waitresses and there is often karaoke equipment for after meal antics.

Please note that most of the restaurants listed in the Non-Chinese Cuisine Section do take reservations and it is advisable to book in advance to secure seating.

At the table

Eating in China is all about enjoying the food. The one thing that novices tend to focus on when starting their China eating adventure is their skill with chopsticks. This consumes their attention to the point that they are oblivious to all of the other intricacies that make up a Chinese meal.

Using a spoon and your chopsticks together is perfectly acceptable for a culinary novice. Many restaurants listed in this guide will have a knife, fork and spoon available

Tip

If you are not skilled with chopsticks, do not make them your primary tools to eat with or you will miss out on all of the incredible tastes and experiences that make up a Chinese meal. Every place setting at a Chinese restaurant comes complete with a small porcelain bowl and spoon. Some of the nicer restaurants even have a metal spoon positioned alongside chopsticks.

if you ask for them. Remember that the real shame is in not enjoying the food, rather than in the way it gets to your mouth.

There is a standard way that Chinese tables are set. Normal settings include chopsticks resting on a small holder, a large plate, a tea cup and a small bowl with a matching spoon inside of it. More upmarket restaurants will have a metal spoon resting on the holder alongside the chopsticks.

In a restaurant with good service, the meal will begin with the waiter or waitress taking the paper cover off of your chopsticks, tucking your napkin under your plate so that it drapes into your lap and offering you tea.

Drinking tea
Tea is typically loose leaf, which means that, as it is poured, you will have floating tea leaves in your cup. The trick to drinking tea with loose leaves is to wait until the leaves have settled to the bottom of your cup before trying to drink it. Gently blowing on the leaves at the top of the cup to move them away from where you are sipping is also acceptable.

A standard teapot is an innocent-looking, small, white porcelain pot. That said, tea pouring is an art in itself. Some restaurants even have Arabian-looking pots with long spouts which come directly from the Silk Road. In the restaurant, one person is employed solely to walk around, pumping the pot to work the water up the spout. This builds up enough pressure to shoot water from a distance into your tea cup. If you would like to participate, you can usually talk this person into letting you try it for yourself. The Chinese enjoy watching foreigners pour water all over their friends.

After the waiter/waitress has poured the first round of tea, the teapot is placed on the table. It is customary to pay close attention to the cups of those sitting nearby and to pour fresh tea for them as their cups empty. When the teapot runs out of hot water, signal to a waiter or waitress to add water by placing the lid of the pot upside down and at a bit of an angle on top of the pot.

When you are served tea by one of your fellow diners, the signal to thank them is to tap your index and middle finger lightly twice on the table.

In a Chinese meal, most dishes are shared in the centre of the table. A meal typically starts with a number of small cold dishes. These are placed on the table first to be nibbled at while the main dishes are being cooked. If there is a large group, a rotating glass disk called a Lazy Susan, placed in the middle of the table, turns constantly so that dishes are available to people sitting around the table.

Etiquette regarding the Lazy Susan involves looking around the table to see if anyone is taking any of the dishes. If not, slowly rotate the dish you desire towards yourself, pausing as it passes other diners and letting them pick what they want.

In a formal situation, everyone will wait for the guest of honour to take the first serving before they begin eating. If the person who seems to be taking charge of the meal spins a dish towards you and offers it, you are being honoured as a guest and should take a serving so that others at the table can also begin eating. If you would like to show your respect to someone else sitting at the table, instead of putting a serving on your own plate, put it on his or her plate.

If eating 'family style', each person uses their own chopsticks to pick food out of a common bowl. In a more formal environment, there are dedicated chopsticks and serving spoons that accompany each dish. You should use these to serve others and yourself, and then eat with your own chopsticks. If you would like to serve another person food using your chopsticks, the polite thing to do is to turn them over and use the end that you are not eating from to serve the other person. To show thoughtfulness to the people eating with you, especially if they are older or in a position of respect, it is usual to serve them before serving yourself.

Most meals are accompanied by rice or noodles. It is customary in China for rice to be one of the last dishes, eaten to top off a meal and fill the empty corners of your stomach. Many visitors to China prefer to have rice as an accompaniment to their meals, as it allows them to enjoy the sauces better. If you do prefer it with your meal, however, you will need to specifically ask the waiter or waitress to bring the rice earlier. Do not be shy about asking for it or it will automatically come at the very end.

When eating a Chinese meal, it is customary to only take small servings of one or two bites at a time. Put the serving into a bowl or on a plate before transferring it to your mouth. Chinese meals are sociable events so when people visit friends and neighbours, food will be the main focus. At very formal events, the restaurant staff may present the food as a whole and then serve individual portions after that.

Cleaning your teeth with a toothpick at the end of the meal is customary in China. The proper way to use a toothpick at the table is to hold it in your right hand and cover your mouth with your left hand so as to keep activity in your mouth personal and more private.

Part way through the meal, waiters or waitresses will bring clean plates and bowls and continually top up your glass, especially if you are drinking beer or wine.

Soup is also served at the end of the meal. A waiter or waitress will present it to the table and then take it away where it will be divided into individual servings. At more basic restaurants, the soup will be placed as any other dish in the middle of the table and you are expected to ladle it into your small bowl and eat with your spoon.

THE ART OF CUTTING FOOD

People accustomed to eating with western utensils always run into difficulty when it comes to cutting food. There are three different methods that can be used to divide food.

• With two hands, plunge your chopsticks into a piece of food and then push each end of the two sticks in the opposite direction to separate it into two pieces.

• Use the edge of your spoon to cut.

• Hold the whole piece up to your mouth, take a bite and return the rest to your plate.

An additional challenge is how to separate meat from bones and shells. In China, it is acceptable to put the whole piece in your mouth, separate the meat from the bone or shell, and spit the bone or shell back onto the plate, or table, via your chopsticks. Forget the years of table manners your mother taught you: when in China, do as the Chinese do.

Aside from tea, Chinese food is often accompanied by soft drinks, juice, beer, local rice wine or western wine. Many Chinese women do not drink alcohol and it is not polite to force alcoholic beverages on them if they prefer soft drinks. Men are a different story and, when eating with Chinese men, it is common for a round of toasts to begin shortly after the meal has begun. It is polite to drink the entire contents of your glass when offered a toast or *gan bei* and when you finish, you should show the person who initiated the toast the bottom of your glass.

Fresh fruit is usually the last thing to be served and comes with a stack of toothpicks. Use the toothpicks to stab the piece of fruit that you want and transfer it onto your own plate. In more upmarket restaurants, a small fork and plate are provided with the fruit.

Getting restaurant staff's attention

In many restaurants listed in this guide, the amount of attention paid to you exceeds that in many other parts of the world. Unfortunately though, in some restaurants in Shanghai, the staff have acquired the unique skill of looking

at you and not seeing you. The reason could be that they are embarrassed or shy about interacting directly with foreigners, although sometimes you are just one more demand at the end of a long day and they simply cannot be bothered.

Either way, the most efficient way to get someone over to your table is to boldly raise your hand. If it is a man loudly say "*Xian sheng*" which is the polite form of mister or sir, and if it is a woman say "*Xiao jie*" which means madam or miss. If they look at you, keep eye contact and continue to motion for them to come to your table. The proper way to motion someone to you in China is by wagging your fingers with your palm facing down, as though you are waving without moving your wrist.

Paying the bill
When you receive the bill, diligently review the items listed, checking the amount of each item and the number of dishes to make sure it adds up to what you ordered. If something seems out-of-line, do not hesitate to ask for a menu to compare what you ordered with what you are being actually billed for.

At the end of a meal, say "Mai dan" to get the bill. You can accomplish the same effect by pretending to scribble something like a signature in the air with your thumb and index finger.

If you are with friends from China, it is customary for there to be a battle at the end of the meal as to who pays. If you are determined to pay the bill, there are a few tricks that can be employed to assure that you win. The best way is to excuse yourself under the guise of going to the bathroom just before the meal ends, and pay the bill.

The second is to be the first person to get hold of the bill. This often involves maintaining encouraging, meaningful eye contact with the waiter or waitress to convince them to deliver it into your hand. The final way is to relentlessly insist on paying the bill. This will probably involve a light skirmish to get it away from the person who has it in hand. If you should lose, heartfelt thanks and the promise of the next meal are the appropriate way to show your appreciation.

TIPPING

The total of your bill will be in renminbi (RMB). It is unusual for a service charge to be included so tipping is not necessary in China. If you do leave a tip, it rarely goes directly to the restaurant staff, but rather reverts back to the owner as part of the revenue for the day or is divided among all staff at the end of the evening.

Leftovers
In China, it is perfectly acceptable to take remaining food home with you. Just ask the waiter or waitress to wrap it up for you to take with you when you leave.

Useful
Chinese
expressions

Hello	Ni hao
Goodbye	Zai jian
Thank you	Xie xie
Yes (to convey something is correct)	Dui
No	Bu dui
I want ...	Wo yao ...
I do not want	Wo bu yao
Good	Hao
Not good / bad	Bu hao
Do you have ...	Ni you ... ma?
Please give me ...	Qing gei wo ...
Don't have	Mei you
How much is it?	Duo shao qian?
Too expensive	Tai gui le
That's enough	Gou le
Sorry / Pardon	Dui bu qi
Where's the toilet? (In most places, just rubbing your hands together to indicate you want to wash them will lead you to a toilet)	Xi-shou-jian zai na li?
Do you take credit cards?	Ke yi yong xin yong ka ma?
Do you have an English menu?	You mei you ying wen cai dan?
Is this spicy?	Shi bu shi la?
I don't want (too) spicy	Wo bu yao (tai) la
I am a vegetarian	Wo shi chi su de
I only want vegetables	Wo zhi yao shu cai
This is very tasty	Zhe ge hen hao chi
This does not taste good	Zhe ge bu hao chi
I would like a receipt	Qing gei wo fa piao

CHINA

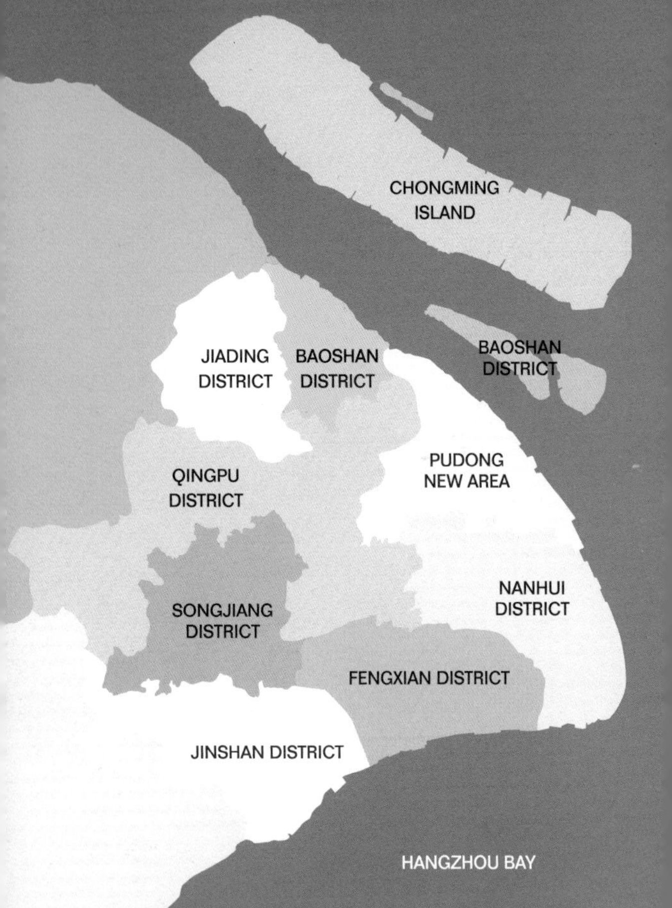

CHONGMING ISLAND

JIADING DISTRICT

BAOSHAN DISTRICT

BAOSHAN DISTRICT

QINGPU DISTRICT

PUDONG NEW AREA

NANHUI DISTRICT

SONGJIANG DISTRICT

FENGXIAN DISTRICT

JINSHAN DISTRICT

HANGZHOU BAY

SHANGHAI

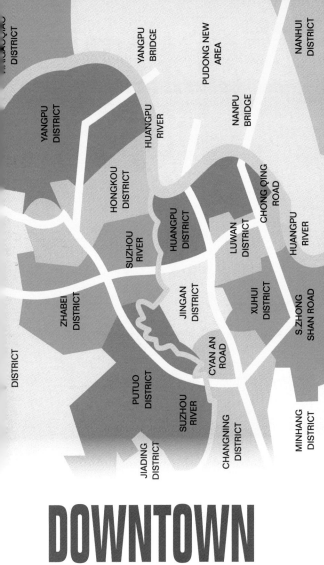

DOWNTOWN SHANGHAI

SHANGHAI METRO

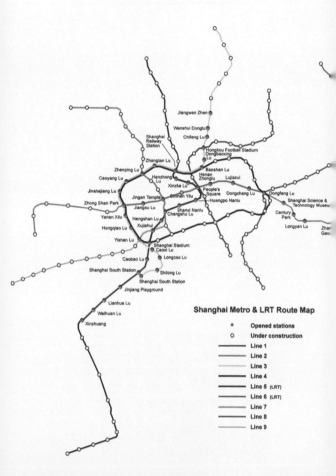

Jiangwan Zhen

Wenshui Donglu
Chifeng Lu
Shanghai Railway Station
Hongkou Football Stadium
Dongbaoxing
Zhongtan Lu
Baoshan Lu
Zhenping Lu
Henan
Hanzhong Zhonglu Lujiazui
Caoyang Lu Lu
Xinzha Lu
Jinshajiang Lu
Jingan Temple Shimen Yilu People's Dongchang Lu Dongfang Lu
Zhong Shan Park Square
Jiangsu Lu Huangpo Nanlu Shanghai Science &
Yanan Xilu Shanxi Nanlu Technology Museum
Hengshan Lu Changshu Lu Century
Hongqiao Lu Xujiahui Park
Longyan Lu Zha
Yishan Lu Gao
Shanghai Stadium
Caoxi Lu
Caobao Lu Longcao Lu
Shanghai South Station Shilong Lu
Shanghai South Station
Jinjiang Playground

Shanghai Metro & LRT Route Map

Lianhua Lu
Weihuan Lu
Xinzhuang

•	Opened stations
○	Under construction
——	Line 1
——	Line 2
——	Line 3
——	Line 4
——	Line 5 (LRT)
——	Line 6 (LRT)
——	Line 7
——	Line 8
——	Line 9

bai cai	cabbage
bai jiu	Chinese white spirit / a grain-based liquor
bai pu tao jiu	white grape wine
bao zi or xiao long bao	steamed dumplings
Beijing kao ya	Beijing duck
bei ke	scallops
bei zi	cup
bian dou	french beans
bing shui	iced water
bo cai	spinach
bo li bei	glass
cai dan	menu
canjin	napkin
cha	tea
chao	stir-fry
chao fan	fried rice
chao mian	fried noodles
chao shu cai	stir-fried vegetables
cha shao	barbecue
cha shao rou	barbecued pork
cha zi	fork
cheng zhi	orange juice
chun juan	spring rolls or egg rolls
cu (pronounced tsu)	Chinese black vinegar
dao	knife
da suan	garlic
dian cai	order
dou fu	tofu
dou ya	bean sprouts
fan qie or xihong cai	tomato
fan qie chao dan	egg and tomato
fan qie jiang	ketchup

GLOSSARY
of foreign terms

gan bei	Cheers! Bottoms up! (This literally means dry glass so you are expected to drink the whole contents of your glass in one gulp)
gan bian	dry fry
gong bao ji ding	chicken cubes with chilli and peanuts
gui hua	osmanthus flower
hai xian	the collective term for seafood
hong cha	black tea
hong pu tao jiu	red grape wine
hong shao niu rou	beef in brown sauce
hong you	chilli oil
hua jiao	Sichuan pepper
hua sheng mi	peanuts
hu jiao fen	pepper
huo guo	hotpot
jiang you	soy sauce
jiao zi or guo tie	pan-fried dumplings
ji dan	egg
ji rou	chicken
jujube	an edible, berry-like fruit
ka fei	coffee
kao	roast
ke le	coke
kuai zi	chopsticks
kuang quan shui	mineral water
la	hot (spicy)
la jiao	chilli
la jiao jiang	chilli sauce
li	pear
li zhi	lychee
long xia	lobster
lu cha	green tea
ma dou	broad beans
mai dan or zhang dan	bill
ma la	the numbing taste of Sichuan pepper
man tou	steamed bread
ma puo doufu or ma la doufu	spicy tofu with minced meat, chilli and Sichuan pepper
mian bao	white bread
mian tiao	noodles
mi fan	steamed white rice
mogu or xiang gu	mushroom
niu nai	milk
niu rou	beef
pang xie	crab
pan zi	plate

pi jui	beer
ping guo	apple
ping guo zhi	apple juice
pu tao	grape
qie zi	aubergine
qing jiao niu rou	stir-fried beef with green pepper
qing zheng yu	steamed fish
re shui or tang shui	hot water
rou	the collective term for meat
shao	braising
sheng jiang	ginger
shui guo	fruit
shui jiao or hun tun	boiled dumplings
suan	sour
su da shui	soda water
tang	soup
tang cu pai gu	sweet and sour ribs
tang mian	noodles in broth
taro	tropical plant used in cooking
tian	sweet
tian suan or tang cu	sweet and sour
tiao geng	spoon
tudou	potato
tudou tiao	crisps / fries
wan	bowl
wei jing	monosodium glutamate (MSG)
wu xiang fen	five spice powder
xia	shrimp / prawn
xian	salty
xian cai	pickles
xiang cai	coriander
xiang jiao	banana
xi gua	watermelon
xi gua zhi	watermelon juice
xi lan hua	broccoli
xue bi or qi shui	lemonade (eg Sprite or 7 Up)
yan	salt
yang rou	lamb
yang rou chuan	lamb kebabs
ya rou	duck
you tiao	fried bread sticks
you yu	squid
yu	fish
yu mi	sweetcorn
zha	deep-fry
zheng	steam
zhi	juice
zhu rou	pork

CHINESE CUISINE

The
sophisticated
east

Shanghai has always been a cosmopolitan and sophisticated city, so it is natural that its cuisine should reflect this. The city is blessed with a year-round supply of fresh food and the local population is able to enjoy fish, shrimp, crab, eel, fowl, water chestnuts, taro, lotus roots, bamboo shoots, bean curd and a wide variety of seasonal greens.

Shanghainese food is traditionally rich, oily, sweet and luscious. Sumptuous and velvety meat or fish dishes are braised with soy sauce, sugar and a touch of vinegar. Shaoxing wine, fermented from glutinous rice, is used extensively in cooking. Many cold 'drunken' dishes are marinated in Shaoxing wine.

Due to rapid development and a sophisticated palate, Shanghai cuisine has mutated to a lighter version with less oil and sugar. While one may go to a restaurant billed as Shanghainese, modern menus will reflect a collection of dishes from all over China. In this way, the restaurants hope to satisfy the discerning tastes of many.

Tip

A Shanghainese meal will start with a large selection of cold appetisers, followed by hot main dishes, hot soups and a sample of xiao chi *(snacks). The meal will end with a plate of assorted fruit.*

Fragrant smoked tea eggs
(cha xun dan)

This dish consists of eggs which are smoked with tea leaves and Chinese five spices. When the eggs are cut into halves and served, the yolk is amazingly rich and liquid, while the egg white retains a crisp clean texture. For those who like smoked flavours, this is a must.

Crisp lotus roots stuffed with glutinous rice
(gui hua tang ou)

Cooked lotus root is stuffed with glutinous rice and flavoured with *osmanthus* flowers. It is then covered with a sugary syrup. Although served as an appetiser, some like to enjoy this dish at the end of the meal as a dessert.

Yellow croaker in wine sauce
(zha xiao huang yu)

Small tender yellow *croakers* are deep-fried then flavoured with salt and wine.

Jujube stuffed with glutinous rice
(nuo mi hong zao)

Jujube beans are pitted and stuffed with slightly sweetened glutinous rice. This dish can be served either cold or warm.

Drunken chicken
(zui ji)

Tender pieces of chicken are parboiled and marinated in Shaoxing wine. Chinese rarely serve boned chicken, so be careful. Once again, it is perfectly acceptable to pick up a large piece, take a bite and put the remainder back on the plate for later consumption.

Crispy garlic eels (zha shan hu)

Small tender eels are deep-fried until crispy. They are then doused in a sweet sauce. Many feel they are addictive and certainly very tasty.

Marinated duck tongue (ya she)

Most duck tongues which are served in China include the Y-shaped bone with the tip of the tongue as a crunchy cartiledge. Braised in a brown sauce with sugar, anise and wine, this is a great dietetic alternative to potato crisps while watching a football match.

Kao fu (kao fu)

This is a vegetarian dish made from bean curd. It has a spongy texture that soaks up all of the wonderful flavours. Usually, it is served with a blend of wood ears, dried golden rod and blanched peanuts, all mixed into a savoury sweet brown sauce.

Cucumber with wasabi sauce (jie mo huang gua)

In this dish, cold cucumber is served in a gentle and mild wasabi sauce. Many people find this particularly refreshing on a hot day.

Mixed preserved bamboo shoots and soy beans (you men sun mao dou)

Pieces of bamboo shoot are mixed with peeled soy beans. They are then served in a light sesame sauce.

Hot meat and seafood dishes

Grandmother's braised pork in brown sauce
(wai po hong shao rou)

This is a fabulous, traditional Shanghainese dish. Pieces of fatty pork are braised in soy sauce, ginger, Shaoxing wine, sugar and star anise. The meat is cooked until the fatty portion falls away at the touch of chopsticks. It can be ordered with hard-boiled eggs in the same sauce. However, do not be put off by the fat. Try to nibble on just a piece to savour the texture and full flavour of this dish. If you are a big meat eater, order the *ti pang* (braised pork knuckles). It is cooked with the same ingredients and comes with many pieces of tender pork.

Stir-fried fresh water shrimp (qing chao he xia ren)

Extremely fresh and crisp, this dish is far better than any shrimp cocktail you have ever tasted! Fresh, small river shrimp are peeled and sauteed over a hot fire in a matter of seconds. It is always served with a dish of black vinegar on the side. Locals will always dip the shrimp in the vinegar for extra flavour, but this does not suit every taste.

Boneless eight treasures stuffed duck (ba bao jiang ya)

With this dish, deboned duck is stuffed with a rainbow of bamboo shoot slices, peas, mushrooms and glutinous rice. The duck is then sliced into pieces and presented on a platter. It is easy to eat and absolutely delicious.

Salt and pepper spare ribs (jiao yen pai gu)

The spare ribs are first marinated in a mixture of Chinese wine, soy sauce, garlic and sesame oil. The pieces are then deep-fried. The ribs are served with a side mixture of salt and pepper. The best way to enjoy this dish is to pick up a rib with your chopsticks or your hands and dip it into the salt and pepper mix for extra flavour. At upmarket restaurants, the ribs are wrapped in foil to make them easier to eat.

Sliced fish fillet in wine sauce
(zao liu yu pian)

Order this dish if you hate fish bones. Sliced white fish is sauteed quickly over a hot fire and mixed with softened wood ears in a mild Chinese wine sauce. The sauce is so delicious that you will need to stand by with a bowl of rice just so that you can pour the remaining sauce over the rice and slurp it all up.

Steamed fish
(qing zheng yu)

Firstly, choose a fresh fish from one of the tanks usually situated at the front of the restaurant. This is better than settling for a fish that has been previously frozen. *Gui yu* (Mandarin fish) is a variety which is tasty for this dish, but there are many choices available. The chef will then prepare the dish by steaming it until the meat is separated from the bones. Sauteed sliced ginger and spring onions are then ladled over the fish. The sauce is simple but some chefs will ladle a spoonful or two of hot chicken fat over it prior to serving to make it tastier. Finally, you can ask the restaurant staff to serve the fish to spare you the trouble of deboning it. When dining with an honoured guest, and in particular if he/she is Chinese, offer them the head and the tail of the fish. These pieces are considered by Chinese to be the most succulent parts of the fish. In particular, the fish cheek is considered a delicacy.

Crab roe with bean curd in clay pot
(xie fen dou fu)

Generous pieces of fresh crab meat and roe are blended with soft chunks of bean curd and slices of ginger to make a thick sauce. This is another great dish to eat with rice.

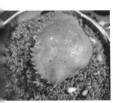

Crab over sticky rice
(pang xie fan)

Pieces of crab are sauteed with scallion and onion, then served over sticky rice.

Crispy skin pigeon
(cui pi ru ge)

If you have never eaten pigeons before, now is the time to try. Do not worry about the cleanliness of the bird as the pigeons served in Shanghai outlets have usually been farmed. Firstly, the bird is marinated in spices, wine and soy sauce before being deep-fried. The pigeon is then cut into several pieces and served on a platter with shrimp chips. It is perfectly acceptable to pick up these pieces with your fingers and gnaw away. You will be pleasantly surprised at how tender and juicy the meat is. Most people particularly enjoy the crispy skin as it is considered to be the best part.

Crispy rice with seafood
(hai xien guo ba)

Shrimp, squid, octopus and wood ears are stir-fried in wine sauce then poured over crispy rice cakes.

Hot vegetable dishes

Stir-fried straw mushrooms with hearts of vegetables (muo gu qing cai)

After eating many meat and seafood dishes, it is good to bite into something pure and simple. The ingredients for this dish are sauteed in oil which has been spiked with garlic. A pinch of sugar and salt completes the seasoning.

Ta cai with winter bamboo (dong suan ta cai)

Ta cai is a flavourful green vegetable that looks like a flat cabbage. Stir-fried with winter bamboo, it is one of the simplest and most memorable vegetable dishes you can order from a Shanghainese menu.

Mashed fava beans and pickled mustard greens (dou ban su)

This dish is the Shanghainese version of mashed potatoes, the ultimate comfort food after a bad day at the office, shopping or sightseeing. Fava beans are peeled, cooked until soft and then mashed. Some people add chopped pickled mustard greens, making it a dish to remember. Not only is it tasty but a great source of fibre and vitamins too.

Seasonal vegetables (shi shu cai)

Ask the restaurant staff for the daily seasonal green vegetable. The choice usually includes *kong xin cai* (hollow vegetable), *bo cai* (spinach), *jian lan cai* (Chinese broccoli), *xi lan hua* (broccoli), *dou miao* (pea shoot) and other seasonal selections. The restaurant staff will ask if you want these vegetables cooked with minced garlic, plain or in a soup base. Take your pick as they are all good.

Tomatoes, soybeans and squash (fang qie mao dou ye kai hua)

While it is best to eat fresh soy beans when in season, they are now available year-round. This is a simple and beautifully presented dish that offers colour, texture, vitamins and lots of fibre.

Celery with water chestnuts (qin cai ma ti)

Another tasty and delicious vegetable dish that combines two crispy ingredients sauteed together with just a pinch of salt and sugar.

Snacks

Pan-fried scallion cakes (cong you bing)

Never the same twice, each restaurant will prepare this dish differently. This is an all-time favourite with the Shanghainese. Spring onions and salt are sprinkled liberally on fresh dough which is then pan-fried to golden brown.

Shanghai stir-fried noodles (Shanghai chao mian)

A quick lunchtime favourite, this is a no frills, stir-fried noodle dish made with pork slivers, dried mushrooms and green vegetables, all mixed with soy sauce and sesame oil.

Vegetables and pork slivers with year cake (ji cai rou si nian gao)

'Year Cake' is a glutinous rice-based pasta that is thickly sliced and then sauteed with pork and vegetables. It is perfect to fill that little space still left in your stomach.

Fried rice
(chao fan)

Rice is mixed with pieces of salted ham, spring onion and scrambled eggs. This dish goes down very well with children who are picky eaters.

Mashed
pumpkin cakes
(nan gua bing)

Mashed pumpkin cakes are a light snack that is delicious, filling and not too sweet.

Small basket buns
(xiao long bao)

Buns are steamed and stuffed with an assortment of pork fillings. They are best dipped in vinegar. Eat them very carefully to avoid clothes stains from the juice explosion when you bite down on the dumpling skin. In fact, it is a good idea to take a small bite of the skin, let the steam escape, suck out the juice, then eat the whole thing.

Desserts

Small glutinous rice balls filled with black sesame
(zhi ma tang yuan)

Small tasty balls that melt in your mouth, this dessert is made from glutinous rice, filled with sweetened black sesame. Each rice ball is cooked in boiling water, then served in a sweet broth flavoured with *osmanthus* flowers. Not only are the texture and taste delicious, but when it is served with small golden flowers floating on the top of the broth, it adds to the magical experience.

Plate of fresh fruit
(shui guo)

Seasonal fruits are always served at the very end of a Chinese meal. Their purpose is to cleanse the palate and aid with digestion.

White lotus pastry (bai guo su)

White lotus nuts are cooked, then mashed with a sweetened mixture and baked in a light and savoury pastry puff.

Soups

Tomato, potato and spare ribs soup (fan qie xiao pai tu dou tang)

A very simple, tasty soup, this is one that always satisfies. The stock is made from spare ribs, ginger, spring onion and salt. Potatoes and tomatoes are added just before serving. Many local diners in Shanghai class this soup as a favourite.

Restaurant listings

1221

1221 Yan An Xi Lu (near Fanyu Lu)

Located in Changning District

021-6213-6585

11:00am–2:00pm, 5:00pm–11:00pm

All major credit cards

This is a perennial favourite of the Shanghai expatriate crowd. Try its drunken crab, *xiang su ya*, beef in spicy broth and *yu xiang* aubergine dishes. The restaurant staff are efficient and helpful, the decor is simple and the food simply good. It is tucked away in an alleyway — just look for the sign 1221 and walk to the end of the alley. Meals cost approximately RMB100 per person.

Bao Luo Restaurant

271 Fumin Lu (near Changle Lu)

Situated in Luwan District

021-6279-2827

11:00am–6:00am

Cash only

This boisterous old favourite of Shanghai locals is always crowded and always a good experience. Meals cost approximately RMB50 per person.

Jade Garden

 388 Zhaojiabang Lu (near Tianyaoqiao Lu)

 Xujiahui   021-6415-9918

 11:00am–10.45pm

   All major credit cards

Excellent service, gracious surroundings and creative dishes make this restaurant a good choice. Meals cost approximately RMB150–170 per person.

Jade Garden

 895 Dalian Lu (near Feihong Lu)

 Xujiahui   021-5595-5385

 11:00am–10.45pm

    All major credit cards

Meals cost approximately RMB150–170 per person.

Lan Gui Fang

 417 Loushanguan Lu (near Xianxia Lu)

 Situated in Changning District

 021-6274-0084

 11:00am–10:00pm

   Cash only

This hole in the wall restaurant is always packed! At lunchtime, people will hover behind you waiting for a seat to eat a bowl of noodles; at dinnertime, be sure to reserve ahead. A small, two-level restaurant, it serves the best Shanghainese noodles in town. Try the various seafood toppings — minced clams, sauteed crab meat or pickled vegetables with *huang yu*. End your meal with a bowl of small black sesame *tang yuan* (a sticky rice dessert). Meals cost approximately RMB50–120 per person.

Lan Gui Fang

🏠 88 South Zunyi Lu, 1st floor of Xie He Building

🧭 Situated in Changning District

☎ 021-6219-9177

🕐 11:00am–10:00pm

💲 💲

💳 All major credit cards

This branch is under the same ownership as that at 417 Loushanguan Lu, but it is newer and bigger. An English menu is available and the food is just as tasty as in the original outlet. Meals cost approximately RMB50–120 per person.

Lu Bo Lang

🏠 Yuyuan Garden, 115 Yuyuan Lu

🧭 Located in Huangpu District

☎ 021-6328-0602

🕐 11:00am–2:00pm, 5:00pm–11:00pm

💲 💲 💲

💳 All major credit cards

Situated next to the zigzag bridge in the Old Town, this is a good place to take a lunch break and order the outlet's sample plate of Shanghainese snacks. Meals cost approximately RMB80–150 per person.

Lu Bo Lang

🏠 Yuyuan Garden, 10 Wenchang Lu

🧭 Located in Huangpu District

☎ 021-6355-0500

🕐 11:00am–2:00pm, 5:00pm–11:00pm

💲 💲 💲

💳 All major credit cards

Meals cost approximately RMB80–150 per person.

Shanghai Uncle

🍳 500 Zhangyang Lu, 8th Floor (near Laoshan Xi Lu)

🧭 Situated in Pudong District

🚇 Dongchang Lu (east exit) 📞 021-5836-7977

🕐 11:00am–2:00pm, 5:00pm–10:00pm

💲 💲 💲 🧾 All major credit cards

Flashy decor and flashy food, this is a fun place for a big celebration. Its eight treasures duck dish is probably the best in town! Meals cost approximately RMB150 per person.

Shanghai Uncle

🍳 211 Tianyaoqiao Lu, 2nd Floor (near Nandandong Lu)

🧭 Located in Xuhui District

📞 021-6464-6430

🕐 11:00am–2:00pm, 5:00pm–10:00pm

💲 💲 💲 🧾 All major credit cards

Meals cost approximately RMB150 per person.

The Grape

🍳 55A Xinle Lu (near Xiangyang Lu)

🚇 Shanxi Nan Lu
(Parkson Exit) 📞 021-5404-0486

🕐 11:00am–Midnight

💲 💲 🧾 Cash only

The Grape caters to the expat crowd, serving delicious Shanghainese home-cooking at great prices. Perennial favourites include *gong bao* chicken, sweet and sour pork and *yu xiang* aubergine. No frills but friendly, this is easily a favourite neighbourhood restaurant. Meals cost approximately RMB60–80 per person.

Xiao Nan Guo

3337 Hongmei Lu (near Yan An Lu)

Situated in Changning District

021-6405-1117

11:00am–2:00pm, 5:00pm–10:00pm

All major credit cards

Offering consistently good food and service, this restaurant is managed with military precision. It is popular both with families and tour groups. Meals cost approximately RMB100–150 per person.

Xin Ji Shi

41 Tianping Lu (near Huaihai Zhong Lu)

Changshu Lu   021-6282-9260

11:00am–1:00am

All major credit cards

This is the original 'Jesse' where the artistic crowd of Shanghai likes to hang out for good food, good conversation and lots of laughs. It is, however, always crowded, smokey and loud. The food served here is undeniably amongst the top ten in Shanghai. Musts to try include crispy rolled cucumber skin, grandma's braised pork, stir-fried beef with *cruellers*, stir-fried river shrimp and crab meat and roe with tofu served in a clay pot. Meals cost approximately RMB50–100 per person.

Xin Ji Shi

 28-3 Taojiang Lu (near Hengshan Lu)

 Located in Luwan District

 021-6445-0068

 11:00am–1:00am

      All major credit cards

Less crowded than the original outlet but it serves the same great food. An excellent place to fill up before hitting the bars around Hengshan Lu. Meals cost approximately RMB50–100 per person.

Xin Ji Shi

 North Block Xintiandi, Building 9, Number 4, Lane 169, Taicang Lu

 Situated near to both Taicang Lu and Huangpi Nan Lu

 Huangpi Nan Lu   021-6336-4746

 11:00am–1:00am

         All major credit cards

Set in an old Shikumen house, this is one of the most reasonable and delicious restaurants in Xintiandi. Reserve ahead for dinner. Meals cost approximately RMB50–120 per person.

Ye Shanghai

 North Block Xintiandi, House 6, Lane 181, Taicang Lu

 Huangpi Nan Lu   021-6311-2323

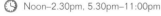 Noon–2.30pm, 5.30pm–11:00pm

 All major credit cards

A beautiful restaurant in the trendy Xintiandi neighbourhood which serves light Shanghai cuisine. Try its drunken chicken, crispy eel, pine nuts with minced chicken served in sesame pocket and baked lamb leg dishes. Dinner costs approximately RMB200–300 per person.

Yin

Jin Jiang Hotel, Gourmet Street, 59 Maoming Nan Lu (near Changle Lu)

Located in the Luwan District

Shanxi Nan Lu   ☎ 021-5466-5070

Noon–2:00pm, 6:00pm–10:00pm

$ $ $ $ All major credit cards

This restaurant has impeccable food, decor and service, plus an impressive wine list. Traditional Shanghai fare is served with flair and mixed with inventive new dishes. Begin your meal with the tofu salad, and do not miss the boneless eight treasures duck dish. Meals cost approximately RMB200–250 per person.

Southern delicacies

The food of the south of China incorporates Guangdong Province (previously known as Canton) as well as Hong Kong. Renowned to be China's finest cuisine (a fact that would be hotly disputed by all other regions of China!), it is probably safe to say it is the most refined of the regional cuisines. The sub-tropical climate of the south provides bountiful fresh fruit and vegetables all year round, which plays a large part in ensuring food from the south is revered by all.

Keep cooking methods simple in order to allow the freshness of the food to shine through. Sauces and spices such as soy, oyster, chilli, hoisin and black bean, are an important part of Cantonese cuisine, and are often served on the side so diners can make their own additions.

There is a Cantonese saying; 'Anything that walks, swims, crawls or flies with its back to heaven is edible'. An updated version of this saying goes; 'The Cantonese eat every thing that flies except planes, every thing on the ground except cars, and every thing that is in the water except boats'.

Pork and duck are the favoured meat dishes in the south, with roasting and barbecuing (*char siu*, meaning 'suspended over fire') being the preferred method of cooking.

The Cantonese have one other distinguishing characteristic when it comes to food — their willingness to try almost anything. Shark's fin, snakes, monkeys and dogs are amongst the least adventurous end of their unusual appetites! In fact, these more exotic types of food are usually only offered in special restaurants. So unless you are looking for this specific type of experience, with the exception of shark's fin, such dishes will be unlikely to show up on your menu.

Cold dishes

Hainan chicken
(hainan ji)

Technically, this dish is not Cantonese but from Hainan Island,
a tropical island off the south of China. This dish will normally
appear in many different types of Chinese restaurants and is
considered to be a healthy option. Chicken is poached in a
broth of spring onion, coriander, salt and pepper, then served
cold with at least two dipping sauces, alongside a bowl of the
poaching stock and a bowl of rice.

Hot meat dishes

Three types of fowl
(san pin)

This is one dish that highlights the Cantonese love affair with barbecued meat. Barbecued duck, chicken and pigeon are served with a dipping sauce.

Crispy chicken
(jiao yan cui ji)

Another barbecued delight, the skin of the chicken is deliciously crispy and the meat succulently tender. A *yin* of salt and pepper and *yang* of soy sauce on the side make a great accompaniment to this popular dish.

Sweet and sour pork
(gu lao rou)

This is the more westernised version where the sauce is made from ketchup, sugar and vinegar. Pieces of tender pork are breaded, deep-fried and sauteed with pineapple and red pepper, then blended with the sweet and sour sauce. A more typical Chinese sweet and sour pork dish would have a dark sauce made from dark vinegar and sugar. Sweet and sour pork ribs are also a Cantonese favourite, easily found in Shanghai.

Stir-fried beef with onion
(cong bao niu rou)

Stir-fried beef with onion is a safe bet if you are not that adventurous. Tender strips of sirloin steak are stir-fried in an oyster sauce and then complemented by sweet red onions which have been cooked until soft.

Hot vegetable dishes

Poached spinach with three kinds of eggs
(shang tang bo cai)

Chinese spinach or a similar green vegetable is poached in chicken broth. A combination of salted egg yolk, thousand-year-old egg and plain old scrambled egg is added to the broth for some variety.

Chinese broccoli in oyster sauce
(hao you jie lan)

Completely different to look at and more bitter than western broccoli, Chinese broccoli is delicious in its own right. It is first blanched in boiling water and then served simply with the oyster sauce either on the side or poured over the top. Both the stems and the leaves can be eaten.

Stir-fried bok choy (chao qing cai)

Bok choy comes in several shapes and sizes; some have long white stems and very green leaves, others are shorter with pale green stems and leaves. Resembling western spinach the most, any number of varieties are available in Cantonese restaurants. The standard method of cooking is to simply stir-fry with some ginger, garlic, sugar and soy sauce.

Soups

Wonton noodle soup (yun tun tang mian)

In China, soup style noodles are far more popular than fried noodles. *Wonton* literally translates to 'swallowing a cloud'. Therefore, the little parcels that appear in this soup usually resemble little clouds. They are commonly filled with pork and shrimp.

Cantonese corn soup (ji rong su mi tang)

A Cantonese classic that is made with creamed corn, chicken and egg white. This soup is slightly frothy and can be surprisingly filling. It is very comforting if you are feeling a bit delicate!

Shark's fin soup (yu chi tang)

Shark's fin is one of the most expensive and prized of all Chinese delicacies. The soup is actually made from a stock of bacon, chicken and beef bones. The shark's fin itself is tasteless and valued more for its apparent medicinal properties.

Crispy noodles with beef (niu rou liang mian huang)

Crispy fried egg noodles are topped with tender beef strips, vegetables and then covered with a velvety oyster sauce. Many people eat the ingredients off the top first and then enjoy the crispy noodles underneath which are covered in oyster sauce.

Fish ball soup
(yu dan tang)

Fish is minced and then formed into small balls, which are poached in a fish stock and served as a soup.

Roast duck noodle soup
(shao ya tang mian)

Pieces of succulent roasted duck are served in an egg noodle soup. A barbecued pork version is also available in restaurants. Many people prefer not to add additional sauces or condiments.

Seafood

Given the wide coastal frontage of the south, it is no surprise that fish and seafood feature regularly in the food from this region. It is fair to say that the south of China is responsible for the Chinese love affair with seafood, which plays an important role in the Cantonese diet. As with all styles of Chinese cuisine, freshness is crucial. Most restaurants have their own tanks from which you can select any number of fish, shellfish and other sea creatures. This section outlines just a few of the different seafood dishes to be found in Shanghai, but often the same cooking methods can also be applied to other types of fish, shellfish and crustaceans.

Seafood sold fresh from tanks in restaurants is usually priced by the *jin* which is actually half a kilogramme. So when you see the price offered for a particular seafood item, remember that it is not for the whole fish, crab etc. It is great fun to chose your own catch, but be careful to check the total price for what you have chosen before it is killed and cooked. Some restaurants have been known to swiftly kill the catch before you have a chance to check what the total cost will be. Speciality items like abalone and lobster can be quite expensive and no Chinese patron will want anything that is already dead, so be sure to insist on checking the weight and price before agreeing to buy.

Steamed mandarin fish (qing zheng gui yu)

One of the simplest and most delicious ways to eat fish is this method. First, choose your fish from the tank. It will then be killed and steamed whole in a marinade of rice wine, soy sauce, chopped ginger and sesame oil. Once cooked, the fish is topped with more finely chopped ginger, black pepper and scallion and a little hot oil is then poured over the top to make the skin crispy. Eat the fish directly off the bone with your chopsticks, and do not forget the cheek meat which is the sweetest part of the fish. Once you have finished eating one side, gently pull the bone away from the tail end as it is considered bad luck to turn the fish over.

Steamed abalone with black bean sauce (dou gu zheng bao yu)

Steamed abalone is served in the half shell with a little sauce, which is a truly delicious way to eat abalone. Add any remaining sauce left in the dish to rice.

Conch with vegetable (xiang luo pian chao shu cai)

Some say that conch is similar in texture to abalone. This dish is simply stir-fried with some celery and carrot to give it a crunchy texture.

Crab fu rong
(fu rong pang xie)

A crab in its shell is broken into pieces then cooked using the same method as lobster *fu rong* (below). Other types of crustacean and shellfish are also often used with this style of cooking.

Razor clams in black bean sauce
(dou gu cheng zi)

China has many, many different types of clams. Razor clams are so named because of their shape. They may look a little different to regular clams but they are just as delicious.

Lobster fu rong
(fu rong long xia)

Fu rong actually means egg white in Cantonese and in recipes it denotes a classic Cantonese cooking method. In this dish, the scallops are coated in a little salt, ginger and rice wine. Egg whites are then beaten until stiff. The scallops are folded into the egg white and then dropped into very hot oil for about 10 seconds until golden brown.

Prawns with heads
(huang jin xia)

The heads of prawns are considered a delicacy in China. In this dish, they are separated from the bodies, both of which are stir-fried in Chinese five spice which makes the bodies very tender and the heads extremely crunchy.

Lobsters in tank
(long xia)

You can choose your seafood, such as this lobster, fresh from the tank.

Restaurant listings

Crystal Jade

Unit 2F-12A&B House 6-7, South Block Xintiandi, Lane 123 Xingye Lu (near Madang Lu)

Situated in Luwan District, a short walk from Huangpi Nan Lu metro station

Huangpi Nan Lu   021-6385-8752

11.30am–11.00pm

                  All major credit cards

Located in the popular and stylish Xintiandi development, always make a reservation at Crystal Jade as it is always packed! The roasted pork belly meat is a must. Depending on how much seafood you order, a meal will cost at least RMB150 per person.

Cu Cai Guan

1697 Xinzha Lu (near Changde Lu)

Located in Jing An District. Take a taxi from Jing An Temple metro station

Jing An Temple   021-6255-3633

10:00am–4:00am

Local credit cards only

Popular with movie star types and regular people, this restaurant is owned by a famous Cantonese film producer. The food puts an unusual spin on the typical Cantonese style. Meals cost approximately RMB100 per person.

Fu Lin Xuan

 37 Sinan Lu (near Huaihai Zhong Lu)

 Situated in Luwan District

 021-6358-3699 / 021-6372-1777

 11:00am–11:00pm

  All major credit cards

Fu Lin Xuan offers high-end delicacies as well as home-style dishes including a good selection of clay pot rice dishes. Order a lot of seafood and a meal could cost RMB300 per person. Order more conservatively and it will total approximately RMB150 per person.

Hengshan Cafe

 308 Hengshan Lu (near Wuxing Lu)

 Located in Xuhui District

 Hengshan Lu 021-6471-7127

 10.30am–3.30am

  Cash only

This outlet serves the simple side of Cantonese food such as barbecued meats, congee and simple stir-fried dishes. Meals cost approximately RMB50–80 per person.

Tongyexuan

 2419 Hongqiao Lu (near Hongjing Lu)

 Situated in Changning District.Take a taxi from Jiangsu Lu metro station

 Jiangsu Lu 021-6268-6705

 5:00pm–10:00pm

  All major credit cards

This is a family style Cantonese restaurant. Meals cost approximately RMB100 per person.

Vale Club

🍴 1088 Yan An Xi Lu (near Panyu Lu)

🧭 Located in Changning District. Take a taxi from Jiangsu Lu metro station

🚈 Jiangsu Lu   ☎ 021-6211-4411

🕐 11:00am–2:30pm, 5:00pm–10.00pm

💲 💲   🖩 All major credit cards

V

Just off the Yan An Lu motorway, Vale Club offers standard Cantonese food in a spacious environment. Meals cost approximately RMB100 per person, without delicacies.

Zen 👨‍🍳

🍴 3/F Hong Kong World Plaza, 283 Huaihai Zhong Lu (near Songshan Lu)

🧭 Situated a short walk from Huangpi Nan Lu metro station in Luwan District

🚈 Huangpi Nan Lu   ☎ 021-6390-6390

🕐 11.30am–Midnight

💲 💲 💲   🖩 All major credit cards

V

Now with a few outlets around the city, Zen started in London and offers consistently good Cantonese food in a modern and comfortable environment. Meals cost approximately RMB200 per person.

Zen 👨‍🍳

🍴 House 2, South Block Xintiandi, Lane 123 Xingye Lu (near Madang Lu)

🧭 Situated a short walk from Huangpi Nan Lu metro station in Luwan District

🚈 Huangpi Nan Lu   ☎ 021-6385-6385

🕐 11.30am–Midnight

💲 💲 💲   🖩 All major credit cards

V

Meals cost approximately RMB200 per person.

Dim sum

Traditionally, Cantonese people eat dim sum for breakfast or brunch, but these days you will find most dim sum restaurants are also open for lunch and occasionally dinner. Dim sum are basically small, one-bite parcels of food that have either been steamed, fried or pan-fried (with the exception of congee which is eaten straight from the bowl with a spoon). The dim sum are generally served in little bamboo steamers or dishes with 2-4 pieces per basket, depending on the particular item.

In traditional dim sum restaurants, large carts laden with bamboo steamers are wheeled around the restaurant and diners pick and choose to their liking. This style of eating is a great way of serving food to people who do not speak any Chinese. However in some restaurants in Shanghai today, you may have to order from a menu. This section of the book should therefore prove useful. As with standard Cantonese cuisine, the condiments are offered separately for you to mix to suit your own preferred taste.

Dim sum restaurants are usually big, loud and lots of fun so enjoy!

A DIM SUM MEAL

- A dim sum meal usually begins by choosing the tea. *Pu er* (black tea), *oolong* (green tea), jasmine or chrysanthemum are popular choices.

- In Cantonese-speaking regions, a dim sum meal is also known as *yum cha* which literally translates to 'drink tea'.

- Tea is definitely the beverage of choice to accompany your dim sum and anyone can refill their cups throughout the meal. If your pot needs a top-up, simply lift the lid to the side so the waiters can see it is empty.

Shrimp dumpling
(xia jiao)

This simple dish is an all-time favourite made up of shrimp and bamboo shoots in a flour-based wrapper. Simple and delicious! These dumplings are usually served in a set of three or four pieces.

Pork dumpling
(shao mai)

Minced pork and shrimp are covered in a flour-and-egg-based wrapper. This is usually served in a set of four pieces.

Glutinous rice with chicken
(nuo mi ji)

Glutinous rice, chicken, reconstituted Chinese dried mushroom, dried shrimp, pork and salted egg yolk are all wrapped in a lotus leaf to form a neat little package. Open up the package and eat the contents but do not eat the lotus leaf. Served in a set of two pieces.

Rice flour rolls
(chang fen)

The wrapper is made from ground rice and water. Traditional fillings include seasoned ground beef, shrimp and barbecued pork. These dishes are served on a plate in a sauce of sweet soy.

Barbecued pork buns
(cha shao bao)

Another favourite which you can eat with your hands but remember to peel off the paper from the bottom of the bun. A chicken version may also be available in some restaurants. Usually this is served in a set of three pieces.

Baked barbecued pork buns
(cha shao su)

This consists of the same filling as the steamed version except it is also wrapped in a flaky pastry and then baked until golden. Usually this is served in a set of three pieces.

Baked turnip pastry
(luo bo si bing)

This delicate and delicious pastry has a savoury filling made from thinly shredded turnip, pieces of salted ham and scallion. It is usually served three pieces per order.

Spare ribs
(dou gu xiao pai gu)

Pork ribs are cut into bite-sized pieces and then steamed with black beans and a little fresh red chilli pepper.

Spring rolls
(chun juan)

Top of the dim sum list is what is known in other parts of the world as the egg roll. However, it is more delicate in both size and taste than the version usually found in the west. The standard filling for *chun juan* is pork, mushrooms and bamboo shoots. Normally, this is served in a set of three pieces, each piece cut in half.

Deep-fried squid tentacles
(zha you yu su)

Some would say this is the Chinese equivalent of calamari. Interestingly, the Chinese idiom to *chao you yu* (fried squid) also means to fire someone!

Hairy taro balls
(zha yu nai qiu)

Do not worry! This dish just
appears hairy but actually, the
coating is very delicate and
melts in your mouth. A set of
three pieces is usually served.

Pan-fried

White turnip cake (luo bo gao)
and taro cake (yu tou gao)

These two dishes are different but actually prepared in the
same way. Turnip or taro is steamed and then mashed. It is
next mixed with a variety of ingredients including dried
Chinese sausage, preserved pork belly, shrimp and Chinese
dried mushrooms.

The mixture is then pressed into baking sheets to set. Once set, it is sliced into pieces and pan-fried. The version from the Zen restaurant also incorporates the establishment's own XO, or chilli sauce. If you do not usually like turnip or taro, try it cooked this way and you will certainly not be disappointed.

Pan-fried mushroom and pork dumplings (guo tie)

A filling of minced pork plus finely chopped Chinese mushrooms and bamboo are enclosed in a rice paper wrapper. The wrapper is then fried in the pan until a little sticky and chewy on the bottom. Many people dip these dumplings in Chinese black vinegar and chilli sauce to taste. Usually this dish comes in a set of three pieces.

Congee (zhou)

Congee is a soup-like dish made with rice. The dish pictured is seasoned with chicken breast and Chinese mushrooms. A variety of different meats and vegetables can be added to the basic rice soup to create different flavours.

CONGEE FLAVOURS

- *Pi dan shou rou zhou* (preserved duck egg congee with pork)

- *Ting zai zhou* (boat congee): squid, peanuts, pigskin, ground beef and fried rice noodles

- *Yu pian zhou* (fish congee): sliced fish

- *Chai yu hua sheng zhou* (dried fish and peanut congee)

Sweet offerings

Egg custard tart
(dan ta)

Dan ta are little pastry tarts filled with Portuguese style egg custard. Normally, three pieces are served in one set.

Mango pudding (mang guo bu ding)

This dessert is similar to its coconut counterpart but made with mango and equally as tasty. Usually it is served as one small dish.

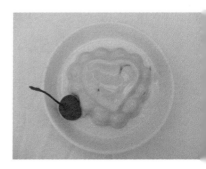

Restaurant listings

Bi Feng Tang

📠 1333 Nanjing Xi Lu (near Tongren Lu)

🚇 Jing An Temple   📞 021-6279-0738

🕐 10:00am–4:00am (weekdays);
8:00am–5:00am (weekends)

💲   💳 Cash only

Bi Feng Tang is a chain of good, inexpensive dim sum restaurants scattered around the city. It serves all your standard dim sum and Cantonese favourites. Particularly good is its roast duck noodle soup. Some of the outlets are open nearly 24 hours making the chain a good option for those in need of a quick, satisfying meal at a strange hour of the day. Meals cost approximately RMB24–45 per person.

Bi Feng Tang

📠 37 Shuicheng Nan Lu (near Gubei Lu)

✪ Situated in Changning District. It is best to take a taxi as this restaurant is not close to a metro station

📞 021-6208-6388

🕐 10:00am–4:00am (weekdays);
8:00am–5:00am (weekends)

💲   💳 Cash only

Meals cost approximately RMB24–45 per person.

Bi Feng Tang

📠 358 Haining Lu (near Wusong Lu)

✪ Situated in Hongkou District

📞 021-6393-5568

🕐 10:00am–4:00am (weekdays);
8:00am–5:00am (weekends)

💲   💳 Cash only

Meals cost approximately RMB24–45 per person.

Bi Feng Tang

 175 Changle Lu (near Maoming Lu)

 Located in Luwan District, near Ruijin Er Lu

 021-6467-0628

 10:00am–4:00am (weekdays);
8:00am–5:00am (weekends)

  Cash only

Meals cost approximately RMB24–45 per person.

Bi Feng Tang

 1/F Golden Magnolia Plaza, 1 Dapu Lu

 Located in Luwan District

 021-5396-1328

 10:00am–4:00am (weekdays);
8:00am–5:00am (weekends)

  Cash only

Meals cost approximately RMB24–45 per person.

Crystal Jade

 Unit 2F-12A&B, House 6-7, South Block Xintiandi Lane 123
Xingye Lu (near Madang Lu)

 Located in Luwan District

 Huangpi Nan Lu 021-6385-8752

 11:30am–3:00pm, 5:00pm–11.30pm

  All major credit cards

Some say this is a more refined restaurant than Bi Feng Tang and therefore more expensive. However, the additional cost is evident in the food and decor. It is located in the trendy, redeveloped old town area of Xintiandi so it is an opportunity for a good meal and the chance to wander through the development afterwards. Its dim sum, which is served at lunchtime only, is excellent and frequented by Hong Kong people living in Shanghai. Meals cost approximately RMB45–90 per person.

Shen Yue Xuan

849 Huashan Lu

Situated a good walk or short cab ride from Jiangsu Lu metro station

Jiangsu Lu   021-6251-1166

7:00am–Midnight

               Cash only

For good dim sum in beautiful, quiet and leafy surroundings visit this branch located inside the picturesque Ding Xiang Garden. Other Cantonese as well as other regional Chinese dishes are also available. Meals cost approximately RMB30–60 per person.

Shen Yue Xuan

4/F Central Plaza, 381 Huaihai Zhong Lu (near Madang Lu)

Huaihai Lu   021-5382-2222

7:00am–Midnight

               Cash only

Meals cost approximately RMB30–60 per person.

Zen at Plaza 66

5F Heng Lung Plaza 66, 1266 Nanjing Xi Lu (near Xikang Lu)

Shimen Lu or   021-6288-1141 /
Jing An Temple   021-6288-1146

10:30am–9:30pm

               All major credit cards

An excellent dim sum restaurant in Puxi's tallest office tower, Plaza 66. It is difficult to isolate a few morsels to pick as favourites as it is all good. However, worth mentioning is the turnip cake in XO sauce. Zen at Plaza 66 is popular with the business crowd at lunchtime but the turnover is quick so you should not have to wait long for a table. Meals cost approximately RMB30–75 per person.

The
spicy west

When most people think of hot Chinese food, they think of Sichuan province and its neighbours, Hunan and Guizhou. Whilst these regions' cuisines are not limited to just spicy dishes, it is definitely what they are renowned for. The spicy flavours found here can be attributed to a liberal use of red chillies in every form; pickled chillies, chilli oil, dried chillies etc. Many of the dishes are not so much hot as mouth numbing and this distinctive taste comes from *hua jiao* (Sichuan pepper).

SICHUAN FLAVOURS

Whilst red chillies and Sichuan pepper tend to dominate Sichuan meals, there are in fact 23 official flavours of Sichuan cookery. Some of the other flavours include:

- *suan la* (hot and sour)

- *ma la* (numb-chilli)

- vinegar

- bean paste

- *yu xiang* (fish flavoured) which ironically does not contain any fish flavouring

It is such a combination of flavours that make Sichuan cuisine so unique and tasty! This can be summed up by the popular Chinese phrase: 'One hundred dishes and one hundred flavours'.

Cold dishes

Sichuan pickled vegetables (pao cai)

Traditionally, Sichuan households were judged by the standard of their pickles. The Sichuan region can be a cold and barren landscape come wintertime and, as with many worldwide areas that share a similar climate, the pickling of fruit, vegetables and meat is an important survival technique.

Sichuan pickled vegetables are not only added to many dishes but can also be served on their own as an appetiser. They will have a vinegary taste that should not be overpowering and are good to pick at with chopsticks.

Shredded chicken and green bean noodles in spicy sauce (ji si la pi)

A variation on the traditional *bang bang* chicken, *ji si la pi* is served on a bed of chilled green bean noodles. Use the noodles to soak up the remaining sauce.

Shredded chicken with sesame paste and chilli oil sauce (bang bang ji)

A variation of this dish is featured on many Chinese menus outside of China. This one, however, should taste quite different. The sauce will be quite thick with a distinctive sesame taste followed by a chilli bite.

Tea smoked duck
(zhang cha ya)

A dish that is not fiery hot, but should taste as it reads with a distinct smoky tea flavour to it.

Finely sliced pork with garlic sauce
(suan ni bai rou)

The pork slices should be almost paper thin, and are in fact referred to as 'lamp shade paper' pork slices. This name suggests you should be able to see the light through them if you go to the trouble of looking!

Fresh cucumber batons in Sichuan pepper and sesame oil
(qiang huang gua)

Do not reach for this dish thinking you are going to cool your taste buds. The cucumbers are actually flash-fried before being served with Sichuan peppers. It is an excellent example of Sichuan cuisine at its simple best.

Hot meat dishes

Fish fragrant pork slivers
(yu xiang rou si)

It is not entirely clear where or when the descriptive term 'fish fragrant' originated. Some say the combined flavours of ginger, garlic, vinegar, chilli and spring onion create a taste similar to that of fresh carp. It has also been said that a crucian carp used to be added to the fermenting brew ... Either way there is nothing fishy about dishes that are labeled 'fish fragrant'. This dish of pork slivers is a particularly well-known Sichuan dish that should please all palates.

Spicy lemon
fish fillet
(xiang la ning yu liu)

Spicy lemon fish fillet is pepper hot as opposed to chilli hot. The pieces of black pepper are visible on the fish and the use of lemon to flavour creates a tasty contrast to the spiciness.

Red braised pork (hong shao rou)

Red braising is rumoured to have been one of Chairman Mao's favourite tastes. Whether this is true or not, it is a delicious method of braising meats using a mixture of dark soy, Chinese wine, brown sugar and star anise. Pork belly, which is poetically known in China as 'five-flower' pork because of its delicate layers of fat and lean, is generally used in this dish. Although too much of it can be quite rich, it is recommended you do not pick around the fatty bits or you will really miss out on the overall taste experience.

Boiled beef slices in a hot sauce (shui zhu niu rou)

This usually comes floating in what looks like a bowl of hot oil and chillies, which is precisely what it is. Pick out the pieces of meat and vegetables and combine with some rice in a bowl. This will take some of the edge off the heat and disperse the oil.

Spicy chicken with peanuts (gong bao ji ding)

Another Chinese classic, a variation of this dish is often served in the west. Although it generally does not have an explosive heat, it will probably be spicier (and tastier) than any outside of China so be careful. Unless you are used to spices, there is no need to eat the actual chillies.

Spicy ribs
(xiang la pai gu)

Pork ribs are seasoned in a spicy coating including salt, pepper and Sichuan pepper, amongst other things, and then deep-fried. A truly succulent dish.

Chilli beef hotpot
(niu rou huo guo)

This mini beef hotpot will give you a taste for the bigger version. However, the bigger version is more of a beef stew which is actually cooked before arriving at your table. By contrast, the mini hotpot is additionally cooked at your table, but this is more for show and to ensure the dish is eaten hot.

Chicken with chillies
(la zi ji)

Again, there is no need to eat the chillies with this dish. Be aware that it can be VERY spicy so try a sample first before digging in earnestly. It is basically Sichuan style Kentucky Fried Chicken!

Hot vegetable and tofu dishes

Stir-fried water spinach with chilli
(qiang kong xin cai)

Many Chinese greens are often not listed on the menu because they are seasonal. Any number of spinach-type vegetables could be substituted here so just ask the restaurant staff what is fresh.

Wrinkle skin green peppers (hu pi qing jiao)

This dish is also known as 'tiger skin' because frying the peppers blisters their skin giving them a stripy look. Within one dish, some of the peppers can be tame in taste and others really fiery so be careful if you get a tame one first as the next one could be a killer! Eat the skin but try to avoid eating the seeds if you want to be safe.

Fish fragrant aubergine (yu xiang qie zi)

As with the fish fragrant pork slivers dish, fish fragrant aubergine contains no fish. By using aubergine with this type of sauce, the flavour completely soaks into the vegetable. It can be a bit oily so it is an idea to mix it with some rice before eating.

Dry-fried green beans (gan bian dao dou)

As this dish is usually served with some pickled black beans and pork mince, it is not considered to be a spicy dish. If you are vegetarian, be careful because often Chinese vegetable dishes such as this one can contain meat. Leaving the meat out of this dish does not really affect the overall flavour but if you are vegetarian, you will have to request for the meat to be omitted.

Spicy Sichuan pepper bean curd (ma po dou fu)

It is fair to say you could judge the standard of the restaurant by its spicy bean curd, a definite Sichuan favourite. Use your spoon to dig deep and always add to rice before eating.

Broad beans with garlic (suan ni can dou)

This dish will only be offered if broad beans are in season which is around May–June. This is a simple and delicious way to eat broad beans. A cold dish of either whole or mashed broad beans cooked in a light chicken stock may also be on the menu, if in season.

Peas and peanuts with chilli (xiang la qing dou hua sheng)

A very interesting combination of ingredients, this dish contains soft sweet green peas which offer a tasty contrast to the crunchy peanuts and spicy red chilli peppers.

Egg noodles with pickled vegetables and various toppings (dan dan mian)

A street food staple in most of Sichuan, this dish is made with egg flour noodles. The noodles are dry not soup-style and usually come sprinkled with pickled vegetables. However, toppings may vary depending on the restaurant.

Spicy cold noodles with chicken slivers (ji si liang mian)

Moist wheat flour noodles are usually used for this dish which incorporates many different flavours. It is topped with blanched bean sprouts that add a tasty crunchy texture.

Sweet dishes

Caramel apples
(ba si ping guo)

Pieces of apple are coated in sugar syrup and cooked until they caramelise. Watch your teeth!

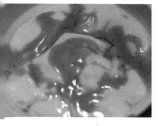

Milky tofu with peanut sauce
(ma rong dou fu)

Sweet, warm tofu with the consistency of custard is mixed with a peanut sauce. Some condensed milk is also added to give a sugary taste, turning the dish into something of a peanut butter milkshake!

Soups

Hot and sour soup
(suan la tang)

A lot of fine black pepper is used in this soup. Somehow, the Chinese vinegar offsets the strength of the pepper a degree, but this dish definitely leaves an impression on your taste buds. It is an excellent soup for warming you from inside out — in a good way.

Restaurant listings

Ba Guo Bu Yi

1676 Hongqiao Lu (near Shuicheng Nan Lu)

Take a taxi to Hongqiao District as there is no metro station nearby

021-6270-6668 / 021-6270-6670

11:30am–2:00pm, 5:00pm–10:00pm

All major credit cards

The restaurant's decor is not as impressive as some, however it does offer solid Sichuan fare. Try the tea smoked duck and mashed broad beans which are particularly worth mentioning. Starters cost approximately RMB5–10. Main courses cost approximately RMB18–25.

Ba Guo Bu Yi

1018 Dingxi Lu (near Yan An Xi Lu)

Take a taxi to Xuhui District as there is no metro station nearby

021-5239-7779

11:30am–2:00pm, 5:00pm–10:00pm

All major credit cards

Starters cost approximately RMB5–10. Main courses cost approximately RMB18–25.

China Moon

🍴 Room 316, 3/F Citic Square, 1168 Nanjing Xi Lu

✪ Located in Jing An District

🚇 Shimen Lu   ☎ 021-6390-6351

🕐 11:30am–10:30pm

💲   💳 All major credit cards

China Moon specialises in Sichuan cuisine but also serves most types of Chinese cuisine. Located in a popular office building in downtown Puxi, the decor is very pleasant, the staff friendly and many speak a little English. Starters cost approximately RMB8–15. Main courses cost approximately RMB20–35.

Pin Chuan

🍴 47 Taojiang Lu (near Wulumuqi Nan Lu)

✪ Situated in Xuhui District

☎ 021-6437-9361

🕐 10:00am–2:00pm, 5:00pm–11:00pm

💲 💲   💳 All major credit cards

Original and authentic Sichuan food is served at this outlet of Pin Chuan. Meals cost approximately RMB100 per person.

Rong Teng Yu Xiang

🍴 171 Pingwu Lu

✪ Located near Huashan Lu

☎ 021-6281-6555

🕐 11:00am–2:00pm, 5:00pm–10:00pm

💳 Cash only

Rong Teng Yu Xiang

 906 Dingxi Lu (near Yan An Xi Lu)

 Take a taxi to Xuhui District as there is no metro station nearby

 021-6212-2511

 11:00am–2:00pm, 5:00pm–10:00pm

 Cash only

Rong Teng Yu Xiang

 275 Jinling Dong Lu

 Situated near Henan Nan Lu

 021-6355-1555

 11:00am–2:00pm, 5:00pm–10:00pm

Cash only

Rong Teng Yu Xiang

 1967 Sichuan Bei Lu (near Changchun Lu)

 Situated in Waitan District

 021-5666-9355

 11:00am–2:00pm, 5:00pm–10:00pm

Cash only

Shu Di La Zi Yu Guan

187 Anfu Lu (near Wulumuqi Zhong Lu)

Located in Xuhui District

021-5403-7684

11:00am–10:30pm

All major credit cards

This restaurant offers not only Sichuan food, but also Dongbei and Hubei. It is decorated in a style similar to a Sichuan village motif. Meals cost approximately RMB50 per person.

South Beauty

5/F Shanghai Times Square, 93 Huaihai Zhong Lu (near Liulin Lu)

Huangpi Nan Lu

021-6391-0890 /
021-6391-0100

11:00am–10:00pm

All major credit cards

Classic Sichuan food is served here in a pleasant setting. All the standard favourites are available but presented in a more sophisticated manner than at a standard Sichuan restaurant. Vegetable and tofu dishes are available at all outlets but if you are vegetarian, check there is no meat inside the dishes you order. Starters cost approximately RMB8–15. Main courses cost approximately RMB20–35.

South Beauty

Unit 1, 28 Taojiang Lu (near Baoqing Lu)

Xujiahui

021-6445-2581 /
021-6445-2582

11:00am–10:00pm

All major credit cards

Starters cost approximately RMB8–15. Main courses cost approximately RMB20–35.

South Beauty

📍 10F Super Brand Mall, 168 Lujiazui Xi Lu (near Yincheng Xi Lu)

🚇 Lujiazui

📞 021-5047-1817 /
021-5047-1917

🕚 11:00am–10:00pm

💲

💳 All major credit cards

V

Starters cost approximately RMB8–15. Main courses cost approximately RMB20–35.

South Beauty

📍 Unit B7-B8, City Centre of Shanghai, 100 Zunyi Lu (near Xianxia Lu)

🧭 Take a taxi to Hongqiao District as there is no metro station nearby

📞 021-6237-2887 /
021-6237-2885

🕚 11:00am–10:00pm

💲

💳 All major credit cards

V

Starters cost approximately RMB8–15. Main courses cost approximately RMB20–35.

South Beauty

📍 881 Yan An Lu (opposite Shanghai Exhibition Centre)

🚇 Jiangsu Lu or Shimen Lu but neither are extremely close

🕚 11:00am–10:00pm

💲

💳 All major credit cards

V

This new branch on Yan An Lu is amazing. Located in an old villa, there has been no expense spared and it takes Sichuan dining (in fact all dining) to a whole new level in Shanghai. Starters cost approximately RMB8–15. Main courses cost approximately RMB20–35 (slightly more at this branch than others but it is worth it just for the decor).

Tony Restaurant

🍴 1121 Zhangyang Lu (near Songjin Lu)

✥ Located in Pudong District

☎ 021-6875-6692

🕐 11:00am–3:00pm, 5:00pm–11:00pm

💲   💳 All major credit cards

V

Tony Restaurant is a chain of restaurants throughout the city serving good standard Sichuan food in a friendly environment. All the dishes listed in this book should be available at this chain and the restaurant staff can sometimes temper the level of spiciness for you if necessary. Starters cost approximately RMB5–10. Main courses cost approximately RMB18–25.

Tony Restaurant

🍴 180 Huayuanshiqiao Lu (near Shiji Dadao)

✥ Located in Pudong District

☎ 021-6887-5028

🕐 11:00am–3:00pm, 5:00pm–11:00pm

💲   💳 All major credit cards

V

Starters cost approximately RMB5–10. Main courses cost approximately RMB18–25.

Tony Restaurant

🍴 16 Wulumuqi Nan Lu (near Hengshan Lu)

🚇 Hengshan Lu   ☎ 021-6467-0777

🕐 11:00am–3:00pm, 5:00pm–11:00pm

💲   💳 All major credit cards

V

Starters cost approximately RMB5–10. Main courses cost approximately RMB18–25.

Tony Restaurant

191 Hongqiao Lu (near Huashan Lu)

Take a taxi to Xujiahui District as there is no metro station nearby

021-6407-7707

11:00am–3:00pm, 5:00pm–11:00pm

All major credit cards

Starters cost approximately RMB5–10. Main courses cost approximately RMB18–25.

**Food from
the north**

Northern cuisine is a hybrid of simple peasant dishes from the countryside, and more refined dishes from the days of the imperial court. An everyday meal is typically heavy on meat and strong in flavour. Soy sauce, garlic, ginger and small leeks are extensively used, and the seasoning is generally not very spicy. Most dishes are braised or stir-fried, with very few steamed dishes.

Even though one will see many offerings of seafood on the menu of a restaurant serving food from the north, the basic emphasis will be on its meat dishes. Lamb, mutton, pork, beef, chicken and duck are prepared in hundreds of different ways, reflecting the contribution and influence of chefs from all over China who were once gathered at the imperial court. Cabbage is the most common vegetable, along with potatoes, aubergine, turnips and a great variety of wild mushrooms.

Rice is also eaten, but the meal is often accompanied by an assortment of steamed or fried breads. A meal is not complete without home-made dumplings and hand-stretched noodles. Food from this region is not out of the ordinary or unique, but the emphasis is rather on delicious dishes made from common ingredients with tastes that are agreeable to the everyday palate.

WHAT TO DRINK

If you want a true northern experience, have a few shots of *bai jiu*, a strong, clear liquor made from grain. On the other hand, warm rice wine is always a mellow match for Chinese food. Soaking a few dried plums in this wine will sweeten it slightly and make it taste like plum wine, which can be drunk throughout the meal.

For those who like their wines very sweet, try the northeastern plum wine which has a similar taste to strong grape juice. When in doubt, beer is always a good accompaniment to the wide variety of flavours in any Chinese meal.

Cold dishes

Traditional style bean curd with shallots
(xiao cong ban dou fu)

Chopped spring onion is mixed with cold tender bean curd bits and blended with a soy sauce, vinegar and sesame dressing.

Northeast hand-stretched potato starch jelly noodles
(da la pi)

A simple and popular starter, this dish blends potato starch jelly noodles with slivered cucumbers in a garlicky, spicy and pungent sauce. It is a bit difficult to pick up the slippery noodles with chopsticks, so scoop it up with your ceramic spoon instead.

Dry wild vegetables (ye cai)

A spicy and flavourful dish, it resembles the look of a weed. The wonderful spicy sauce has you going back for seconds.

Edible fungus (liang ban mu er)

Wood ears are blended with a mild soy sauce, vinegar and garlic dressing. The texture is soft and crisp at the same time.

Empress dowager's beef (ci xi tai ho niu rou)

This dish contains sliced preserved beef with hints of five-spice flavouring.

Candy vinegar Chinese cabbage mound (cu liu bai cai)

Chinese cabbage is pickled and served with a pungent sweet and sour sauce.

Boiled peanuts
(shui zhu hua sheng)

Plain boiled peanuts are served in brine and star anise. Pick up two peanuts at a time and you are on your way to becoming a chopstick expert. This is a favourite snack to accompany drinks.

Harbin sausage
(ha er bin xiang chang)

The secret ingredients of this delicious pork sausage come from the northernmost province of Heilongjiang. This dish can be sliced and eaten as an appetiser or as an accompaniment to drinks.

Slivered duck mixed with green bean jelly
(ya si fen pi)

Slivers of duck meat and cucumber are mixed with green bean jelly and dressed in soy sauce, garlic and vinegar. This is another slippery dish to master with chopsticks, but worth the effort.

Hot meat dishes

Beijing duck
(Beijing kao ya)

Firstly, the duck is cleaned and air is pumped under the skin to separate it from the flesh. Then, the duck is coated with a mixture of oil, sauce and molasses. It takes approximately 40 minutes to roast the duck until the skin turns golden brown and crisp while keeping the meat tender. The duck is presented whole to the diners before being sliced at the tableside where the crispy skin is served separately from the meat. Hot, thin flour pancakes are served in steamers alongside the duck meat.

How to eat Beijing duck

- Take one pancake and place several slices of meat and skin in the centre.

- Next, dab some plum sauce called *tianmianjiang* over the meat and skin.

- Add slivered spring onions and/or slivered cucumbers to taste.

- Roll up the whole pancake and eat with your fingers.

Boiled pickled Chinese cabbage and pork
(chuan bai rou)

This clay casserole dish combines pickled Chinese cabbage and slivers of pork in a savoury broth. Typically, it is classed as a main soup dish, with the pickled Chinese cabbage lending a naturally pungent taste. Scoop it into a bowl with plenty of broth and enjoy.

Sun island flaming dragon fish (tian suan long yu)

This dish is a house special at the Dong Bei Ren restaurant chain. The fish is first fried then covered with a sweet and sour sauce. To complete the experience when dining at Dong Bei Ren restaurants, the restaurant staff will serve it whilst singing a delightful folk tune about how the fish is prepared.

Stir-fried mutton with spring onions (cong bao yang rou)

Marinated, thinly-sliced mutton is stir-fried quickly over a hot fire and blended with lots of sliced spring onions. A popular dish with the locals, it is good either by itself, scooped over rice or stuffed in a baked sesame bun. Best to eat it piping hot.

Stewed chicken and mushrooms (xiao ji dun mo gu)

Pieces of chicken are stewed with wild mushrooms and potato starch jelly in a light brown sauce. Served in a clay pot, this is another local favourite.

Willow of duck in a nest
(ya si yao guo)

Sauteed duck slivers with green peppers, red peppers, cashews and onions are served with a spicy sauce and presented in a nest of deep-fried string potatoes.

Cod in pumpkin shell
(xue yu nan gua)

Boneless cod is braised in a slightly sweet brown sauce and served in a small pumpkin. It is not only creative but equally delicious.

Hot vegetable dishes

Stir-fried Chinese cabbage in sweet and sour sauce
(cu liu bai cai)

Chinese cabbage is sauteed with black vinegar and a touch of sugar.

New style stewed potato and aubergine
(qie zi dun tu dou)

A favourite, tasty combination in the northeast of China, this simple dish is both flavourful and comforting.

Bean curd in stone pot
(dou fu bao)

Fried bean curd squares are braised with mushrooms and vegetables in a brown bean sauce and topped with shrimp and broccoli spears. This dish is served in a delicate black stone pot that preserves the heat.

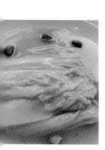

Chinese cabbage with chestnuts in saffron juice
(hong hua zhi li zi bai cai)

Braised Chinese cabbage with cooked chestnuts is served in a savoury light sauce infused with saffron.

Vegetables with mushrooms
(qing cai mo gu)

Fresh, green seasonal vegetables are served, accompanied by three different kinds of mushrooms. All ingredients are cooked in a mild chicken broth stock.

Snacks

Hand-stretched pancakes (zhua bing)

Use your fingers to tear apart this slightly greased and salted pancake. You will find it comes apart in the same way that thick pieces of string do.

Fried pancakes with beef and turnips (niu rou luo bo xian bing)

Minced beef and chopped turnips are mixed with mild spices. The mixture is then stuffed into a dough pastry and pan-fried until golden brown on both sides. Filling and delicious, this also makes a great breakfast food.

Maize porridge
(yu mi zhou)

A local favourite, maize porridge fills in the corners of the stomach.

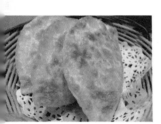

Big baked leek cake
(jiu cai he zi)

Leek, bean thread and slivered egg pieces are chopped finely and stuffed into a thin dough pastry that is pan-fried. Eat it carefully as the filling can be very hot and greasy.

Baked corn pancakes
(da bing zi)

A typical northeastern snack, this is made from cornmeal.

Dumplings
(jiao zi)

This dish is a plate of mixed *jiao zi* with different fillings and wrappers. Dip each one into the pre-made sauce of garlic, soy sauce and vinegar.

Soups

Emerald fish soup
(fei cui yu tang)

This enticing green soup is made from finely chopped fish, green vegetables and almonds and is served in a light broth. The chopped almonds add a special touch.

Hot candied apple
(ba si ping guo)
and Hot candied bananas
(ba si xiang jiao)

Pieces of apples and bananas are deep-fried and coated with sugar syrup. When this dessert is served at the table, pick up a piece and dunk it in a bowl of cold water. This will create the *si*, or threads of sugar syrup. This dish is a perennial favourite for all those with a sweet tooth!

Home style crisp fried egg dough
(su huang cai)

Flat pieces of egg dough are deep-fried and coated with sugar syrup. Dunk the pieces in cold water and enjoy a crispy light treat.

Restaurant listings

Dong Bei Ren

46 Fanyu Lu (near Yan An Xi Lu)

Located in Changning District

021-5230-2230

11:00am–10:00pm

Cash only

Fun and colourful decor, Dong Bei Ren serves inexpensive and tasty meals. Order the sweet and sour fish and a singing waiter will serve it to your table. Also try the various potato starch dishes, savoury pastries and boiled dumplings. Meals cost approximately RMB40–80 per person.

Dong Bei Ren

1 Shanxi Nan Lu (near Yan An Zhong Lu)

Shanxi Nan Lu   021-5228-9898

11:00am–10:00pm

Cash only

Meals cost approximately RMB40–80 per person.

Dong Bei Ren

555 Shuicheng Lu (near Maotai Lu)

Situated in Changning District

021-6233-0990

11:00am–10:00pm

Cash only

Meals cost approximately RMB40–80 per person.

Lao Bei Jing

 1 South Henan Lu (3rd floor Xing Ten Building)

 021-6373-4515

 11:00am–2:00pm, 5:00pm–10:00pm

  All major credit cards

This outlet is slightly more upscale than the other restaurants in town. The decor, service and presentation of food are all impeccable. Meals cost approximately RMB80–150 per person.

Ya Wang

 20 Tianyaoqiao Lu (near Zhaojiabang Lu)

 Xujiahui

 021-6464-9169

11:00am–11:00pm

  All major credit cards

Besides very good Beijing duck which is served tableside, the menu has numerous northern dishes and a column of Shanghai favourites. Inexpensive and noisy, this restaurant serves consistently good food and good fun. Meals cost approximately RMB50–100 per person.

Zhuang Jia Yuan

 215 Kangping Lu (near Huashan Lu)

 Xujiahui

 021-6282-3612

 11:00am–11:00pm

 Cash only

This is a small, folksy restaurant serving authentic northeastern fare. Try the *la pi*, a spicy cold dish. Inexpensive and casual, this tiny gem is a great find in a city full of large restaurants. Meals cost approximately RMB30–60 per person.

From across
the straits

Taiwan cuisine offers an abundant choice of seafood, snacks, rice and pasta dishes. As it is a semi-tropical region, there is also a huge selection of shaved ice and smoothies, all made with fresh fruits. Most dishes have absorbed the flavours and ingredients from mainland China, however, Taiwan food still shines with its distinctive freshness and variety.

Cuttlefish, oysters, shrimp, clams and squid are creatively cooked in stir-fried dishes, snacks and soups. They are also chopped and blended to make flavoured 'balls'. Pork is minced, diced or slivered. It can also be breaded, and deep-fried as whole chops served over noodles.

Shallots are a key ingredient in most stir-fried dishes. Typically, they are sliced thinly then sauteed lightly in oil. Next, they are mixed in with other ingredients to give the slight garlicky and sweet taste. Fresh coriander is often finely chopped and sprinkled on top, while Thai basil gives the 'Three Cup' dishes their unique taste which is unlike any found in other Chinese dishes.

Freshly squeezed juices, smoothies and *choua bin* (shaved ice) should be a part of any Taiwanese meal.

Starters

Tofu with preserved egg
(pi dan ban dou fu)

Tender cold bean curd, mixed with thousand-year-old eggs, is sprinkled with Taiwanese pork shred and served with a sweet Taiwanese thick soy sauce. As this dish is hard to handle with chopsticks, it is advisable to dig in with your ceramic spoon.

Taiwanese cold cut trio
(Taiwan san ping)

This dish is an attractive combination of three cold favourites — shredded seaweed, preserved bean curd and stewed eggs.

Taiwanese pickled cabbage
(Taiwan pao cai)

Pickled cabbage, carrots and turnips are served in a sweet and vinegary dressing.

Lettuce roots with sesame sauce
(liang ban wo sun)

Finely slivered lettuce root is mixed with salt, sesame oil and crushed Sichuan peppercorn. The result is a light and crunchy starter.

Hot seafood and meat dishes

Stir-fried beef with Chinese crullers
(you tiao niu rou)

Sliced beef is stir-fried with *you tiao*, Chinese fried crullers in oyster sauce.

Home-made southern Taiwanese style minced pork
(lu rou fan)

Minced pork with pieces of fatty meat is stir-fried with shallots, sesame oil and soy sauce. This dish is best eaten over a bowl of rice. In some restaurants, *lu rou fan* can be ordered as part of a set menu that includes soup and fruit.

Hakka-style stir-fried home dish (ke jia xiao chao)

Squid, celery, preserved bean curd, spring onion, fresh chilli peppers and shallots are quickly stir-fried for this tasty dish.

Three flavoured potted chicken (san bei ji)

Also known as Three Cup Chicken, the chicken is braised for about half an hour in equal portions of soy sauce, cooking wine and dark sesame oil. Ingredients also added include whole garlic cloves, slivers of ginger and sprigs of spring onion. Thai basil is mixed in at the last moment. This is a dish bursting with flavour that is sure to please.

Shrimp stuffed Chinese doughnut with pineapple (bo luo you tiao xia)

Bits of shrimp are stuffed into pieces of Chinese fried dough stick and blended with mayonnaise and chunks of pineapple. A new invention of a recent vintage dish that is a favourite amongst foreigners and children.

Chinese cabbage dried fish and scallop (gan bei bian yu bai cai)

Chinese cabbage is cooked in chicken broth until it reaches a very soft consistency. It is then flavoured with dry bits of fish and scallops. This is another great dish for ladling over the rice bowl.

Fried oyster with egg (ou a jian)

Oysters and eggs are a favourite combination amongst Taiwanese.

Green onion sauce over steamed chicken (cong you ji)

Spring onions are ladled over simply steamed tender chicken pieces sauteed in hot fragrant oil. Dip the pieces in chilli paste or sweet soy sauce for more taste.

Tofu and vegetable dishes

Taiwanese fried bean curd (tai shi zha dou fu)

Tender *dou fu* pieces are cut into squares then deep-fried until the outside is crispy. They are then served with a sweet and sour sauce. This dish is at its best eaten very hot before the crispy skin softens.

Stinky bean curd (chou dou fu)

Stinky *dou fu* is certainly an acquired taste. As with blue cheese, the more you eat it, the more you like it. Dip this dish in chilli paste, ignore the smell and enjoy the complex taste.

Stir-fried assorted mushrooms
(hui chao jun gu)

An assortment of cultivated and wild mushrooms are sauteed together.

Stir-fried seasonal vegetables
(shi shu)

Ask the restaurant staff for the seasonal vegetable list. All vegetables can be ordered stir-fried *qing chao* (simply), *suan ni* (with garlic) or *shang tang* (in a broth).

Spicy beef noodles
(hong shao niu rou mian)

Originally imported to Taiwan from mainland China, spicy beef noodles has become the signature noodle dish of Taiwan. The beef stock has a hint of star anise, and the noodles are served with large chunks of beef/and or beef tendon. Side dishes of chopped pickled mustard greens and coriander are served as an accompaniment, and should be mixed in with the noodles. A meal in itself, this dish is very hearty and spicy.

Pork bean sauce over noodles
(za jiang mian)

Minced pork, finely minced garlic and chopped spring onion are all stir-fried and mixed with sweet bean paste. The mixture is then poured over freshly made hand-stretched noodles.

Taiwanese stir-fried homemade pancakes
(tai shi chao bing)

Pan-fried dough pancakes are cut in large slivers and stir-fried with shallots, spring onions, assorted vegetables and pork.

Taiwanese stir-fried rice noodles
(tai shi chao mi fen)

This dish consists of rice noodles which have been stir-fried with dried shrimp, shallots, mushrooms and roasted pork.

Fresh shrimp fried rice served in pineapple
(xian xia bo luo chao fan)

The traditional-style fried rice is dressed up with pork shreds which are sprinkled on top. The dish is served in a fresh pineapple shell.

Soups

Clam and ginger soup
(jiang si and ge li tang)

Slivers of ginger are blended with chopped clams and cooked in a light broth.

Pork ball soup
(gong wan tang)

Tangy pork balls with a crispy texture are served in a bone broth laced with pieces of celery, turnip and spring onion. Also try the fish ball soup, squid ball soup or a bowl of mixed ball soup.

Drinks

Fresh fruit and vegetable juices (xin xian shui guo shu cai zhi)

Almost all authentic Taiwanese restaurants offer a large selection of fresh fruit juices and fresh vegetable juices.

Papaya milk (mu gua niu nai)

Fresh papaya is blended with milk to make a filling and refreshing drink.

Tapioca pearl milk tea
(zhen zhu nai cha)

This Taiwanese classic consists of sweetened tea with milk and served with many chewy tapioca pearls.

Desserts

Smoothies
(bing sha)

The word *bing sha* translates to 'ice sand'. Try this delicious and refreshing dessert in the following flavours: peanut, fresh guava, fresh pineapple, sesame, taro, peanut and coffee, fresh mango and fresh strawberry. The best idea is to order several together and share with everyone at the table.

Shaved ice with toppings (choua bin)

This dessert is a mountain of shaved ice, a douse of condensed milk, plus any of the following toppings: red beans, green beans, peanuts, tapioca pearls, taro and/or fresh pineapple. A real treat to fight those hot and humid days in Shanghai, one *choua bin* can easily be shared by four people.

Restaurant listings

Bellagio (Lu Gang Xiao Zhen)

 101 Shuicheng Nan Lu (near Hongqiao Lu)

 Located in Changning District

 021-6270-6865

 11:00am–4:00am

 All major credit cards

As this restaurant is always crowded, a reservation is recommended. Fantastic mango smoothies, combination shaved ice and numerous noodle and dumpling dishes are popular. Meals cost approximately RMB50–80 per person.

Bellagio (Lu Gang Lao Zhen)

778 Huangjin Cheng Dao (near Gubei Nan Lu)

Situated in Changning District

021-6278-0722

11:00am–4:00am

All major credit cards

Meals cost approximately RMB50–80 per person.

Charmant (Xiao Cheng Gu Shi)

1418 Huaihai Zhong Lu (near Fuxing Xi Lu)

Changshu Lu   021-6431-8107

11:00am–4:00am

All major credit cards

Good food and excellent service, this is Taiwan fare at its best. Choose from an extensive menu including stir-fried dishes, Taiwanese favourites such as *niu rou mian*, *guo tie*, shaved ice and smoothies. Meals cost approximately RMB50–80 per person.

Ding Tai Fung

Peace Square, 12-20 Shuicheng Lu (near Hongqiao Lu)

Located in Changning District

021-6208-4188

11:00am–2.30pm, 5:00pm–11:00pm

All major credit cards

Famous for its thin-skinned *xiao long bao* and other steamed pastries, this Taiwanese restaurant has a clean modern decor and professional restaurant staff. The menu is limited to mostly snacks and soups. Try the crab meat *xiao long bao*, steamed vegetarian dumplings, chicken soup and assorted cold appetisers. Meals cost approximately RMB100–150 per person.

Kuo Bee Pen Da

301-1, Huashan Lu (near Changshu Lu)

Situated in Xuhui District

021-6249-8877

11:00am–2:00pm, 5:00pm–4:00am

All major credit cards

This Taiwanese hotpot restaurant also serves traditional island fare.
Meals cost approximately RMB60–100 per person.

Kuo Bee Pen Da

689 Shuicheng Lu (near Tianshan Lu)

Situated in Hongqiao District

021-6229-5449

11:00am–2:00pm, 5:00pm–4:00am

Local credit cards only

Meals cost approximately RMB60–100 per person.

Kuo Bee Pen Da

567 Zhaojiabang Lu (near Xiaomuqiao Lu)

Located in Xuhui District

Xujiahui   021-5496-1431

11:00am–2:00pm, 5:00pm–4:00am

Local credit cards only

Meals cost approximately RMB60–100 per person.

The silk road

Officially named Xinjiang Uyghur Autonomous Region, Xinjiang covers most of the north-west region of China. The area borders Mongolia, Russia, Kazakhstan, Kyrgyzstan, Tajikistan, Afghanistan, India and Tibet. Whilst there are many Han Chinese living in Xinjiang these days, the Uyghur people are the region's native inhabitants. Indeed, Xinjiang and its native people have little in common with the rest of China in terms of appearance, language, culture and tradition, not to mention food.

Pork, which is such a staple favourite throughout the rest of China, is not found in Xinjiang as the Uyghur people are Muslim. Mutton, however, is plentiful. It is considered to be the region's preferred meat although you will find some beef, chicken, duck and a little fish as well.

The food which originates from Xinjiang is hearty and filling with bread, meat, rice and root vegetables featuring frequently. It also makes use of spices that do not appear in Chinese cuisine, such as cumin.

Tip

Xinjiang is also famous for its grapes and the serving of fresh fruit after a meal is perhaps the closest thing that this region's cuisine has in common with the typical Chinese style.

Snacks

Lamb kebabs
(yang rou chuan)

By far the most famous of Xinjiang snacks, lamb kebabs are chunks of fatty and lean lamb skewered on a wooden stick and roasted over a spit. They are then seasoned with salt, lots of red pepper and cumin. Lamb kebabs prove to be delicious when bought straight from a street vendor at 2:00am.

Nan bread
(nang)

Truly, nan bread is the staple bread of Xinjiang cuisine and a crucial part of the Uyghur diet. The word 'nan' originates from the Persian language and this type of bread is popular throughout the Arabic and Middle Eastern world. While there are different varieties of nan, the basic method of cooking

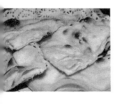

it is by sticking dough to the inside wall of an extremely hot oven. Then, after a few minutes, remove the cooked bread. The shape of the bread is typically round, flat and golden brown. Other varieties include *younang* (oil nan), *zhimanang* (sesame nan) and *rounang* (mutton nan).

Xinjiang bagels

Not exactly the same as those heralding from New York, but this variety run a close second!

Cold dishes

Cold vermicelli (la pi)

Cold, thick rice noodle vermicelli is served with black vinegar, topped with chilli sauce and fresh coriander. Once you have finished the noodles, soak up the tasty leftover sauce with some rice.

Xinjiang salad
(liang cai)

Xinjiang food features some great salads that taste extremely fresh. This salad dish will vary from restaurant to restaurant but should include ingredients such as garlic shoots, wood ear fungus, bamboo and sesame oil.

Tiger salad
(lao hu cai)

It is unclear where the tiger reference fits in but this is a great salad full of fresh ingredients which are rarely served raw in Chinese cuisine. It is a salad of finely sliced red onion, tomato, coriander, carrot, red pepper, all soaked in a sesame oil dressing.

Eighteen savouries salad
(shi jin liang cai)

The real thing probably features the full 18 ingredients but these days in might be scaled down a bit. This dish should include ingredients such as red pepper, bean sprouts, carrots, wood ear fungus, celery, beans, spinach and enoki mushrooms. Again, all of the ingredients are served uncooked.

Hot meat dishes

Dapan chicken
(dapan ji)

This dish literally translates as 'big pan of chicken', and not surprisingly consists of a large dish of chicken pieces, lots of chilli, plus potatoes and shallots. It is sometimes served with large flat noodles which you can use to mop up the sauce.

Lamb ribs yili
(yang rou yili pai gu)

Lamb ribs are deep-fried and served with a crunchy, slightly spicy coating.

Zirin chicken
(ziran ji)

This is also available as a lamb dish but for those who need a bit of variety, order the chicken. It features boneless cubes of chicken fried in the Xinjiang spices of cumin and chilli flakes. Salt and pepper is also added.

Lamb with nang
(nang bao rou)

Combining two of the regions favourite ingredients, this dish is similiar to a lamb stew with sauce served on top of Xinjiang flat bread. The bread does a great job of soaking up the sauce.

Roast mutton
(kao yang rou)

Roast mutton is as famous in Xinjiang as roast duck is in Beijing and crispy suckling pig in Guangzhou. A two-year-old sheep

is first slaughtered and skinned, then daubed with salt inside and out, and then coated with a mixture of eggs, chopped ginger, scallions and pepper. The sheep is put into a stove to roast for about an hour until it turns golden brown. Whole roasted sheep are usually available at most Xinjiang restaurants. However, if you have enough people and wish to order one, you should do so in advance. If you just want a taste rather than the entire sheep, roasted legs are usually available without prior notice.

Lamb pie
(yang rou bao)

Another lamb dish but this time it is prepared as a peppery lamb stew with potatoes encased in a thick pastry crust.

Rice and noodles

Pulled noodles
(lamian)

Witnessing the making of these noodles is truly an amazing experience. Watch chefs pull the noodle dough by hand to create thinner and thinner strings until finally the strands are about the thickness of spaghetti. The noodles are then boiled quickly and various ingredients are added, including oil, mutton pieces, cooked tomato, egg and chilli peppers. A stir-fried version called *chao lamian* is also available in some restaurants.

Ding ding noodles
(ding ding mian)

Noodles are first chopped into pieces about three centimetres long, then stir-fried in a sauce of tomato and lamb.

Hot vegetable dishes

Potato cake
(tudou bing)

This flat cake of shredded fried potato is served with a sprinkling of chopped peanuts and lots of salt and fine black pepper on top. It is both simple and delicious!

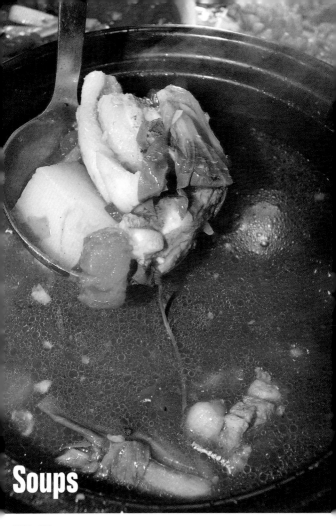

Soups

Xinjiang soup
(Xinjiang tang)

Not just a simple tomato soup, this dish is also cooked with pieces of pasta, lamb and various vegetables. It is also referred to as 'a meal in a soup'. One bowl as a snack is certainly filling enough.

Restaurant listings

Qiu Zi Gu Li

🍳 255 Dongzhuanbang Lu (via Jiangsu Lu)

🧭 Situated a short walk from Jiangsu Lu metro station in Changning District

🚇 Jiangsu Lu   📞 021-6210-1977

🕙 11:00am–11:00pm

💲 💲   📕 Cash only

A good choice for standard Xinjiang dishes, this restaurant is also set in a pleasant environment. A lamb kebab barbecue is set up at the front so order a couple of sticks to satisfy your hunger whilst waiting for your table as it is consistently busy. You can book the private rooms if you are in a party of six or more, otherwise you will just have to try your luck. Recommended is the Dapanji and the salads. Meals cost approximately RMB50–70 per person.

Uighur Restaurant

🍳 1 Shanxi Lu (via Yan An Zhong Lu)

🧭 Located in Luwan District, just a short walk from Shanxi Nan Lu metro station

🚇 Shanxi Nan Lu   📞 021-6255-0843

🕙 10:00am–11:00pm

💲 💲   📕 Cash only

The food here is adequate, but be prepared to dance. There is a stage with live performances throughout the night and the restaurant staff can be quite persistent in encouraging patrons to get up and join in. Perhaps you might want to order a Xinjiang black beer as soon as you arrive to work up the courage to perform! All the dishes are good. Meals cost approximately RMB60–90 per person.

Yakexi

 688 Nanjing Xi Lu (opposite Shanghai TV station)

 Situated near to Shimen Lu metro station in Jing An District

 Shimen Lu   021-6217-4774

 11:30am–10:30pm

 Cash only

A friendly restaurant which offers wholesome Xinjiang food. There is also a lamb kebab stall out the front if you do not have the time or hunger for a full dining experience. If you have a group, call in advance and book the whole roasted mutton as it is a speciality and very tasty. However, you may not want to eat mutton or lamb for a while afterwards! Meals cost approximately RMB50–80 per person.

Hotpot for a
cold night

The ultimate social meal has to be sitting around a big table with a steaming pot of boiling liquid in the centre, surrounded by plates of meats, fish, seafood, vegetables and sauces.

The Chinese hotpot boasts a history of more than 1,000 years. The original version contains thinly sliced raw mutton. This is first cooked in a hotpot, which has been placed in the middle of the table and filled with boiling water. The mutton is then gently dipped in a sauce before being eaten.

Modern versions of this Chinese fondue have also evolved. Diners can choose from variations in the choice of boiling stock, the type of raw food to be cooked and the type of mix-it-yourself sauce to be added.

In Shanghai today, one can find different types of hotpot restaurants from Mongolian/Beijing to Sichuan/Chongqing and even Hotpot Nouveau.

Mongolian/Beijing style

Traditional Mongolian style hotpot is made from clear stock, and flavoured with pieces of mushroom, dried shrimp, crab and assorted herbs and spices. Many restaurants of this type choose to use traditional, funnel-shaped copper pots that hold burning coal in the centre. It is possible to order plates of thinly sliced beef, lamb/mutton, fresh live shrimp, along with fresh or frozen bean curd, Chinese cabbage, a variety of mushrooms and green vegetables. The sauce is usually pre-mixed, but you can order additional bits of coriander, spring onion, garlic and barbecue sauce. Traditionally, baked buns, corn congee and dumplings are eaten as an accompaniment to the hotpot ingredients.

At the end of the cooking feast, the meal is rounded off with a bowl or two of the delicious stock (this makes for a fabulous risotto stock, so take it home with you).

Drink the lethal white spirit called *mao tai* to accompany the meal, or try a milder version of Chinese rice wine which is normally served warm. Drink the rice wine out of a ceramic bowl for the full experience. All types of beer go well with this meal but grape wines are not recommended.

Sichuan/Chongqing style

Just as the cuisine from Sichuan/Chongqing is very spicy, so too is the hotpot. The broth is flavoured with chilli peppers and other pungent herbs and spices. Hot peppers, crystal sugar and wine are just some of the main ingredients used in this hotpot.

If you want to experience both mild and spicy, it is possible to order a *yuan-yang* pot. This comes with two sections; one containing a spicy broth, and the other a milder clear stock. A selection of typical raw foods to be cooked would include sliced meats, kidneys, beef tripe, goose intestines, eel, sea cucumber, assorted bean curd products and a wide variety of vegetables.

Lots of beer, pitchers of freshly squeezed watermelon juice and bottles of water are a must with this meal.

Hotpot nouveau

This style of hotpot has been coined by the authors themselves and describes a new style of restaurant emerging in Shanghai. Originally started by mainly Taiwanese restaurateurs, these outlets offer the greatest variety of ingredients for stocks, raw food and sauces.

The choice of stock for this style of hotpot can vary between the traditional clear chicken broth, fish head broth, curry based broth and Thai style hot and sour stock. For those who prefer two types of stock, it is possible to order one pot divided into two sections.

Raw ingredients include sliced beef, lamb, chicken, fish, shrimp, fish balls, cuttlefish balls, shrimp balls, dumplings, fried dough sticks, soft bean curd, frozen bean curd, dried

bean curd, many varieties of mushrooms, green vegetables, lotus roots, various types of wheat pasta, green bean vermicelli and rice pasta.

Diners also have the option to make their own sauce from a large selection at a nearby cart. Choose from soy sauce, wine, vinegar, minced ginger, minced garlic, chopped spring onions, chopped coriander, along with fermented bean curd sauce, peanut butter sauce, sesame paste, XO sauce, satay sauce, fresh chillies, chilli paste, chilli oil, sesame oil — the selection is endless. If you are a novice at this style of eating, ask the restaurant staff to prepare a sauce for you. With a little experimentation, you will soon be able to mix the perfect sauce by yourself.

A delicious drink with this style of meal is iced chrysanthemum tea with honey which is both cooling and refreshing. Pitchers of freshly squeezed juices and bottles of Qingdao beer are perfect partners too.

Restaurant listings

Coca Suki Hot Pot

 Raffles City, 268 Xizang Zhong Lu (near Fuzhou Lu)

 People's Square  021-6340-3182

🕐 10:00am–10:00pm

  All major credit cards

At this chain of restaurants, you will find Thai style hotpot, excellent service and a clean atmosphere. Meals cost approximately RMB100 per person.

Coca Suki Hot Pot

Unit 604-605, City Centre of Shanghai, 100 Zunyi Lu (near Xianxia Lu)

Located in Changning District

021-6237-2686

10:00am–10:00pm

Cash only

Meals cost approximately RMB100 per person.

Hot Pot King

10 Hengshan Lu (near Gao An Lu)

Hengshan Lu   021-6474-6545

11:00am–4:00am

All major credit cards

Sichuan/Chongqing style of fare is served at Hot Pot King. Meals cost approximately RMB80–100.

Kuo Bee Pen Da

Unit 1, 301 Huashan Lu (near Changshu Lu)

Located in Xuhui District

021-6249-8877

11:00am–2:00pm, 5:00pm–4:00am

All major credit cards

This is certainly the place to come for a great variety of raw foods, sauces and stocks. Meals cost approximately RMB60–100 per person.

Kuo Bee Pen Da

689 Shuicheng Lu (near Tianshan Lu)

Situated in Changning District

021-6229-5449

11:00am–2:00pm, 5:00pm–4:00am

Local credit cards only

Meals cost approximately RMB60–100 per person.

Kuo Bee Pen Da

567 Zhaojiabang Lu (near Xiaomuqiao Lu)

Situated in Xuhui District

021-5496-1431

11:00am–2:00pm, 5:00pm–4:00am

Local credit cards only

Meals cost approximately RMB60–100 per person.

Sunny Red Hot Pot Village

857, Zhongshan Nan Er Lu (near Wanping Nan Lu)

Situated near Shanghai Gymnasium

021-6438-4269 /
021-5424-9003

10:30am–Midnight

Cash only

The Sunny Red Hot Pot Village serves Beijing style fare with an emphasis on lamb and beef, all set in a colourful decor. Meals cost approximately RMB40–80 per person.

Sunny Red Hot Pot Village

 482 Jinhui Lu (near Wuzhong Lu)

 Located in Minhang District

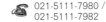 021-5111-7980 / 021-5111-7982

 10.30am–Midnight

  Cash only

Meals cost approximately RMB40–80 per person.

Tan's Fish Head

 400 Guilin Lu (near Tianling Lu)

 Situated in Xuhui District

 Caobao Lu   021-6408-5118

 9:30am–11:00pm

  Yin Liang card only

The highlight of this restaurant is that it has a good selection of stock bases. Meals cost approximately RMB50–80 per person.

Wu Ji Mala Hot Pot

 Room 011, Concord World Plaza, Yongyuanbang Lu (near Zhenning Lu)

 Situated in Jing An District

 021-6248-4723

 11:00am–3:00am

  Cash only

Sichuan/Chongqing style fare is available here. Meals cost approximately RMB30–40 per person.

Wu Ji Mala Hot Pot

691 Xianxia Lu (near Anlong Lu)

Situated in Changning District

021-6290-4518 /
021-6291-5028

11:00am–3:00am

Cash only

Meals cost approximately RMB30–40 per person.

Wu Ji Mala Hot Pot

90 Hongsong Lu (near Jinhui Lu)

Situated in Minhang District

021-6402-1790 /
021-6402-4445

11:00am–3:00am

Cash only

Meals cost approximately RMB30–40 per person.

Shanghainese snacks

In Shanghai, snacks and street food are so abundant and delicious that it is actually a crime not to try something new at least once a day.

Take an early morning stroll through the local streets and you will see steamed buns, pan-fried dumplings, sesame balls, sweet and savoury fried cakes, fried dough sticks, sticky rice-filled dumplings and steaming bowls of noodles and wontons. Inexpensive and yummy, breakfast is picked up by many locals on their way to work. Snacks are also eaten throughout the day or ordered at the end of a meal to 'fill-in the empty pockets of the stomach'. For a local experience you will never forget, try the snacks described below.

Steamed snacks

Sticky rice dumplings
(shao mai)

For those familiar with dim sum from the south, this street dish is the Shanghai version of *shao mai*. Instead of pork and shrimp filling, it is stuffed with sticky rice cooked in soy sauce and flavoured with mushrooms and bamboo shoots. It is advisable to eat this snack with lots of napkins as the juice will run out as soon as you bite into it.

Little basket buns (xiao long bao)

THE most famous Shanghai snack, these small buns are filled with minced pork and spices, then steamed in bamboo steamers. Eat with chopsticks or push a bun into a Chinese ceramic spoon and eat. Try not to break the skin and be careful when you eat it as the hot juice will squirt out and ruin your clothes. The trick is to take a tiny bite first, suck out the meat juice, then confidently pop the whole small bundle into your mouth. This is delicious plain, or eaten with black vinegar, a dash of chilli sauce and a touch of slivered ginger if you prefer. When you are browsing through the Old Town District, you are likely to see the long queue by the zigzag bridge. Many people feel it is well worth queuing for over an hour in order to buy a styrofoam container of ten little basket buns.

Little basket buns with crab meat (xie fen xiao long bao)

For a gourmet touch, try this variation of little basket buns. The addition of crab meat to the minced pork makes it even more tantalising. The snack portion of most restaurant menus will feature these buns as it is common to eat them at the end of a meal.

Large steamed buns (bao zi)

This snack is a fresh, hot steamed sandwich eaten on the run. It is difficult to decipher the bun fillings as they tend to look alike when they come out of the steamer. It is therefore advisable to have some knowledge of Chinese so that you can ask. *Rou bao* is minced pork, *cai bao* is chopped green vegetables mixed with mushrooms and *dou sha bao* is a sweet red bean paste filling. One renminbi will normally buy you breakfast for two and these buns are great for taking home and popping in the freezer. Whenever the munchies hit, wrap one in plastic film and microwave for one to two minutes for a tasty quick snack.

Sticky rice with fried stick (ci fan)

If you are a fan of *fan*, this snack is for you. Sticky rice is wrapped around a freshly deep-fried stick of dough. Eat with your fingers and enjoy the combination of naturally sweet rice and crunchy dough.

Boiled sticky rice flour dumplings (tang yuan)

Made from sticky rice flour, the dough for these dumplings is slightly sweet and chewy. In most outlets, it is possible to order either a savoury minced pork filling, or a tasty sweet filling of black sesame or red bean paste. This is served in a bowl of hot water and dotted with a sprinkling of *osmanthus* flowers.

Meat or shrimp small wontons (xiao hun tun)

This version of wontons is more delicate than the larger version called *cai rou da hun tun*. The filling can be either minced pork or minced shrimp, or a combination of the two. *Xiao hun tun* are, of course, best when fresh, but wontons can easily be purchased in the frozen food section of most supermarkets and kept at home for a quick snack.

Vegetable and meat big wontons (cai rou da hun tun)

This is truly a meal in itself anytime of the day. Chopped vegetables are mixed with minced pork and flavoured with wine, soy sauce and slices of ginger wrapped in thin wonton skins. Next, the skins are boiled until they float up in the pot. They are then ladled into a clear broth which has been dotted with chopped spring onion, pickled mustard greens, dried seaweed and slivered egg pancakes. One bowl of these wontons can easily induce a two hour nap.

Vegetable and meat dumplings (jiao zi)

Jiao zi is the Chinese equivalent of ravioli. It is at its best when the dough is hand-rolled, with the centre of the dough thicker than the edges. When made in this way, the texture is chewier, similar to home-made pasta. There are literally hundreds of fillings to choose from. A popular choice is Chinese cabbage with minced pork, but also try chopped tomatoes and minced beef, or shredded carrots and turnips.

Jiao zi are often eaten by dipping them in a sauce of black vinegar, garlic and chilli paste.

There are many regional differences in the preparation of this snack. For example, the Shanghainese version is small and delicate whilst the northern version is denser and bigger. If you want to be adventurous, there are speciality dumpling shops dotted around Shanghai where you can try a wide variety of these boiled goodies.

Fried snacks

Deep-fried sticks
(you tiao)

You tiao is one of the most common breakfast foods on the streets. They are crunchy, greasy and absolutely scrumptious. Eat this foot long stick in a variety of ways; by itself, stuff it in sesame bread, cut it into small pieces and eat with congee, stuff it with shrimp and serve as a dish, wrap sticky rice around it for a snack or cook it in a hotpot as a crunchy addition.

Twisted crispy snack
(da ma hua)

Dough is twisted, deep-fried and sprinkled with lots of sugar. The texture is not soft like a doughnut, but instead quite crunchy. This makes a great mid-afternoon snack with a hot cup of *cha*.

Spring roll
(chun juan)

The *chun juan* found in Shanghai should not be confused with the burrito-sized ones found in the United States and Europe. Shanghainese spring rolls are much daintier, and meant to be dipped in vinegar and chilli paste then eaten with fingers. The Shanghainese version is also often vegetarian. Standard spring rolls contain cabbage, bamboo shoots and mushrooms, whilst fancier ones are made with pieces of slivered pork and shrimp. Instead of eating these tiny morsels as appetisers, as one would in a Chinese restaurant abroad, those in Shanghai are enjoyed after the main dishes have been served. They act as a filler in case one is still hungry. Spring rolls are popular buffet finger food at parties and once you have tried these small gems, you will never return to the big mammas.

Sesame balls
(ma qiu)

Sesame balls are the perfect food to bring a smile to your face. This racketball-sized snack is made from sticky rice flour, with a sugar or red bean paste filling. The outside is covered with fresh sesame seeds. Fried to a golden brown, this snack is hard to resist. However, be careful if you buy one directly from the frying pot. It is a good idea to bite gently and let the hot air escape first!

Mashed pumpkin cakes
(nan gua bing)

Fresh pumpkins are first mashed then coated with sticky rice dough. A filling of red bean paste or *jujube* bean paste is added, and the cake is fried gently to a golden orange. *Nan gua bin* make an unforgettable dessert or snack.

Pan-fried snacks

Bottom fried small buns
(sheng jian man tou)

Walk along any local street in the morning and wherever you see a queue is where these buns are sold. They are simple buns stuffed with meat and beautifully arranged on a large, rimmed pan. This is then placed over an open fire for the buns to cook. When they are almost done, the chef will sprinkle sesame seeds and chopped spring onion over the buns. The bottom of these little jewels are crusty, while the top is soft and the meat filling juicy. However, they are also messy to eat so take care when biting into them. To order, one has to usually buy a ticket at the cashier before standing in line. This snack is sold in ounces with four buns equalling one ounce. Therefore, you will have to tell the cashier how many ounces you want to buy as opposed to how many buns. The going price is about one renminbi fifty fen per ounce. A word of advice is to eat these fresh on the spot as re-heating makes them too chewy.

Bottom fried
dumplings
(guo tie)

Boiled dumplings are bottom fried for a crunchy texture. Dip them in soy sauce and vinegar, and eat with chopsticks.

Baked snacks

Slivered turnip puff cake
(luo bo si su bing)

Turnip is finely slivered, mixed with spring onions and a pinch of minced ham, and wrapped in Chinese puff pastry. It is then baked until light golden brown. This snack is a surprisingly delicious food, even for those who normally do not like the flavour of turnips.

Baked egg custard tart
(dan ta)

An egg custard mixture is wrapped in pastry dough then baked

to perfection. This small dessert serves one and is rich but not overly sweet. It is best eaten as soon as it leaves the oven and is still hot. Typically a southern dim sum, *dan ta* have become very popular on the streets of Shanghai. They are sold in most bakeries, and even in the Kentucky Fried Chicken chains all over China.

Congee

Plain congee
(zhou)

You are not a novice if you like *zhou*. This plain rice soup mixture is served with pickled cucumbers, fermented preserved bean curd, dried pork and salted peanuts. This snack is marvellous for those who grew up eating it, but very few adventurous eaters take to it on the first try.

Thousand-year-old
egg and pork congee
(pi dan zhu rou zhou)

A morning wake-up call, a light midday meal or a hot filler after a night out on the town, a bowl of congee is the supreme comfort food.
Thousand-year-old egg and pork congee is only one of many variations on the theme of *zhou*. Congee is in fact rice that has been cooked in about ten times the usual amount of water. The mixture becomes literally a rice soup. Any and all bits can then be added, including plain chicken or *ji zhou*. The authors' favourite is sliced fish *zhou* with freshly chopped spring onions, a sprinkle of sesame oil and thin slivers of fresh ginger.

Noodles and other pasta snacks

Did Marco Polo bring back noodles from China? We will never know for certain, but many suspect that he did. Noodles in China come in so many varieties that we could write a whole book on all the different types of noodles and other pasta dishes available. Choose from wheat noodles, rice flour flat noodles, green bean vermicelli, rice stick noodles, potato starch noodles, just to name a few. The method of making them also varies from machine-made, hand-made, hand-stretched or cut by a knife directly into a boiling pot of water. Noodles in China are either served in a soup or stir-fried.

Pickled mustard greens and pork noodles in broth
(zha cai rou si mian)

This is probably the most popular Shanghainese noodle dish. First, the noodles are cooked in boiling water, then ladled into a large ceramic bowl containing clear chicken or bone broth. This broth is usually flavoured with chopped spring onions and white or black pepper. A serving of stir-fried mustard greens and pork is then heaped on top. If you are not too proficient with chopsticks, eating this dish can prove to be quite a task as the noodles are very long. With the help of a ceramic spoon, you will probably make only a small mess after some practice. Chinese will typically eat a bowl of 'long-life noodles' on their birthday instead of a piece of cake.

Dan dan noodles
(dan dan mian)

Originally from Sichuan, the Shanghai version of *dan dan* noodles is slightly milder but still spicy. Wheat noodles are mixed with minced pork, garlic, spring onion and flavoured with sesame paste, peanut butter, soy sauce, cooking wine and vinegar. Chopped peanuts are sprinkled on top. This dish can be served completely dry, or with a small amount of broth.

Minced pork with sweet bean sauce over noodles (zha jiang mian)

Minced pork is stir-fried with garlic and scallion, then mixed with sweet bean sauce. The sauce is freshly prepared and then poured over cooked noodles. Slivered cucumbers and blanched bean threads can be sprinkled on top for a crunchy texture. This dish is a favourite comfort food for many Chinese.

Crab meat noodles (xie fen lian mian huang)

Thin wheat noodles are cooked al dente and pan-fried on both sides. Next, a magical mixture of fresh crab meat, ginger and spring onions is poured over the top.

Spring onion and dried shrimp noodles (cong you kai yang ban mian)

A favourite amongst the Shanghainese, these simple wheat noodles are sprinkled with sesame oil and soy sauce. They are then mixed with a generous portion of stir-fried spring onion and dried shrimp which has been cooked until almost crisp. These noodles are typically eaten at the end of the meal.

Beef noodles soup
(niu rou mian)

Considered to be one of the best noodle soups available, this dish originated in Taiwan. A stock pot of beef, tendon and bones, with soy sauce, cooking wine, anise, sugar, chilli peppers, garlic and ginger, are cooked over a simmering fire for many hours.

Fresh, hand-made noodles are quickly cooked al dente, then ladled into a large bowl. Pieces of green vegetables are placed on top, and a healthy portion of the beef and tendon stock poured over. This is served with chopped spring onions and pickled vegetables on the side. If desired, these can also be thrown into the bowl to make the broth even more flavourful. Once again, eat carefully with your chopsticks and ceramic spoon.

Singapore rice noodles
(xing zhou chao mi fen)

A popular dish throughout Southeast Asia, these curry flavoured rice noodles will please even the most discerning palate. The authentic version will contain roasted pork, shrimp and onions, and have slivers of egg pancakes on top. However, every restaurant has adopted its own recipe for this dish. Peter McCarthy, author of *McCarthy's Bar*, rated the Chinese restaurants around Ireland by how well they prepared this dish.

Seafood rice noodles
(hai xian mi fen)

Shrimp, squid and scallop are stir-fried with scallion and mixed in with rice noodles. For extra flavour, seafood rice noodles can be eaten with a slightly sweet tomato based sauce.

Drinks

Soy bean milk
(dou jiang)

Last but not least, an unforgettable experience in Shanghai is to drink soy bean milk from street vendors. A favourite breakfast drink, soy bean milk is freshly made every morning by pressing soy beans. It can be sweetened with sugar, or served savoury in a soupy mix of pickled mustard greens and dried seaweed. This is then sprinkled with sesame oil. Not only is this drink good for you but it tastes fantastic!

Restaurant listings

Cang Lang Ting

689-691 Huaihai Zhong Lu (near Sinan Lu)

Shanxi Nan Lu   021-5382-3738

6.30am–10:00pm (1st floor), 11:00am–8:00pm (2nd floor)

Cash only (1st floor). All major credit cards (2nd floor)

Cang Lang Ting offers a great selection of Shanghainese noodles with various toppings. Meals cost approximately RMB20–50 per person.

Ding Tai Fung

1/F Peace Square, 12-20 Shuicheng Lu (near Hongqiao Lu)

Situated in Changning District

021-6208-4188

11:00am–2:30pm, 5:00pm–11:00pm

All major credit cards

This restaurant is famous for its Taiwanese-style *xiao long bao*, which many think are the best in the world. The skin of the *xiao long bao* served here is extremely thin, and the filling less fatty but very juicy. Meals cost approximately RMB100–150 per person.

Nan Xiang

Yuyuan Garden, 85 Yuyuan Lu (near the zigzag bridge)

Situated in Huangpu District

021-6355-4206

7:00am–8:00pm

All major credit cards

Line up next to the zigzag bridge in Old Town to get a taste of Shanghai's famous *xiao long bao*. Meals cost approximately RMB10–30.

Street vendors

Shanghai streets are full of small vendors selling snacks and noodles. Be adventurous! There are also many snack and noodle chain shops that provide inexpensive snacks in a clean environment. These are too numerous to list individually, but below are some of the major ones.

Cang Lang Ting

Wu Yue Ren Jia

Both these outlets are well-known for serving great noodles.

Da Niang Shui Jiao

This is a favourite for *jiao zi* (boiled dumplings).

Ji Xiang Hu Tun

Jin Shi Fu

For *hun tuns* (wontons), these are two good chains.

Yong He Da Want

Xi Nian Lai

Yi Jian Yi (also known as 1+1)

For a good variety of Taiwanese noodles and snacks, these three outlets are firm favourites.

You Liang Sheng Jian

Feng Yu Shen Jian

For Shanghainese favourites such as *xiao long bao* (steamed little basket buns) and *sheng jian bao* (bottom fried buns), try these two chains.

The above listed outlets are similar to those of McDonalds and Burger King in that they are located in every district and are too numerous to list individually. To find them, consult the concierge at your hotel or ask local friends to direct you.

There are also streets in Shanghai which are dotted with restaurants and food stalls serving a great variety of food. For a bit of local colour and flavour, try one of the following:

- Huanghe Lu

- Nujiang Lu

- Yunnan Lu

- Zhapu Lu

- Hongmei Lu Pedestrian Street

Eating
vegetarian

If you are a vegan, then Shanghai will feel like paradise. Chinese vegetarian dishes display a harmonious balance of colours and textures as well as flavours. The creative use of bean curd, roasted seaweed, hundreds of varieties of mushrooms, fungus, gluten and nuts is unrivaled in vegetarian cuisine from anywhere else. Whether inside a Buddhist temple or on the ever-packed Nanjing Road, these vegetarian restaurants will astonish you with their taste, variety and low-cost.

One of the oldest and most famous vegetarian restaurants in town is Gong De Lin. Founded in 1922, this State-run establishment is still going strong. The menu is extensive, and covers over 25 cold dishes and 100 hot dishes.

A new kid on the block, the outlet Vegetarian Lifestyle (also known as Zao Zi Shu), markets its restaurant as a lifestyle choice. 'No Alcohol, No Meat, No Egg, No Smoking' is the motto. Here, the food is lighter and brighter without sacrificing taste. To complement the food, there is also an extensive choice of healthful teas and freshly squeezed fruit juices.

MOCK MEATS

Do not mock the 'mock meats' until you have actually tasted them. One bite of *gong bao* mock chicken will certainly change your mind and a plate of sweet and sour mock pork will have you scrutinising the ingredients.

These meats not only taste like the real thing, but they look like it too. Even if mock ham is not your cup of tea, you can stick to the infinite varieties of bean curd and fresh vegetable dishes available.

Cold dishes

Three types of strips in hot sauce
(san si la pi)

This spicy sauce is a beautiful blend of green bean jelly, carrots and cucumber. Lots of sesame paste, garlic and peanut sprinkles are added to the flavour and texture.

Hand roll
(shou juan)

Shou juan is a variation of the Japanese hand-roll containing alfalfa sprouts, bean sprouts, carrots, lettuce and rice all wrapped in a crispy roasted seaweed skin. Dip it into a dish of traditional wasabi and soy sauce, and eat it with your fingers.

Barbecued duck
(gua lu kou ya)

Thin bean curd sheets are rolled together, braised in a light brown sauce, then cut into bite-sized pieces. It does not actually taste like duck, but is nevertheless wonderful with a chewy texture.

Tofu skin roll
(dou fu juan)

This tasty dish is made with chopped green vegetables and chopped nuts, all rolled up in a thin, tasty *dou fu* skin. Usually, it will be cut and neatly served in bite-sized pieces.

Ham
godly style
(gong de huo tui)

Ham godly style is smoked mock ham made from pressed bean curd and served wafer thin.

Pickled
cabbage
with hot taste
(chuan la suan cai)

Pickled cabbage is chopped and mixed with red hot pepper and served in a slight sweet and vinegary dressing.

Chicken and cashews
(yao guo ji ding)

Shanghai serves a better version than the original. There is no chicken, but plenty of cashew crunch and a perfect blend of chilli peppers and seasoning.

Assorted casserole
(nuan dong ju hua guo)

A light clay pot dish made with sliced thin bean curd, bamboo shoots, carrots and seasonal vegetables. It is served in a vegetable broth mixed with green bean threads. Scoop the mixture into a small bowl and savour the sweet broth.

Fillet of pork with salt and pepper
(jiao yen pai tiao)

Mock pork made from strips of lotus root is deep-fried then sprinkled with a mixture of pepper and salt. It is usually served with fresh sprigs of coriander.

Mock minced crab meat
(xie fen)

A signature dish at the Gong De Lin restaurant, this dish is normally served in a ceramic crab shell. Finely minced carrots are mixed in with a cooked type of grain called *xiao mi*. This imitates the taste of crab meat and crab roe.

Smoked beef
(yan huo niu rou)

Wrapped in foil and flambeed at the table, this gluten-based mock beef dish is served mixed with sliced bamboo shoot. It is a fine imitation of the real thing.

Stewed mixed vegetables in casserole
(luo han bao)

A blend of different mushrooms, ginkgo nuts, broccoli, carrots and bamboo shoots are mixed in brown sauce and served in a clay pot.

Lamb skewers
(yang rou chuan)

Mushrooms are skewered, deep-fried and finally seasoned with lots of sesame seeds and cumin. Close your eyes and you might think you are eating lamb!

Soups

Pumpkin soup
(nan gua tang)

Pumpkins are mashed and cooked with vegetable broth to make this delightfully light soup.

Minced corn soup
(yu mi tang)

Finely chopped corn mixed with vegetable broth makes this a simple ending to any meal.

Snacks

Vegetarian buns
(cai bao)

The vegetarian version consists of steamed buns with chopped vegetables and mushroom filling. It is perfectly acceptable to eat these with your fingers.

Steamed vegetable dumplings
(cai jiao)

Finely chopped green vegetables are wrapped in a *jiao zi* wrapper and steamed in small bamboo steamers. Dip the dumplings into chilli paste and vinegar to add more taste.

Stir-fried noodles
(san xian mian)

Typical of Shanghainese style, these noodles are stir-fried with green vegetables, mushrooms and sprouts, then flavoured with soy sauce and sesame oil.

Desserts

Longans and lotus in soup
(guai yuan lian xin tang)

This dessert is a smoked and oolong-flavoured sweet soup containing longans and lotus. Be careful of the longan pits.

Drinks

In more established vegetarian restaurants, the usual assortment of soft drinks, beers and Chinese wines will usually be available. In the new breed of vegetarian restaurants, alcohol has been replaced by freshly squeezed fruit juices and a long list of herbal and healthful teas.

Restaurant listings

Gong De Lin

🛎 445 Nanjing Xi Lu (near Chengdu Bei Lu)

🚇 People's Square   ☎ 021-6327-0218

🕐 11:00am–2:00pm, 5:00pm–9:30pm

💲 💲   💳 All major credit cards

 🇻

Since it opened over 80 years ago, Gong De Lin has consistently served Shanghai traditional vegetarian fare. Try the particularly delicious mock ham, mock duck and fish in wine sauce. Go with a crowd as the menu boasts over 200 selections. Meals cost approximately RMB60–120 per person.

Vegetarian Lifestyle

🛎 258 Fengxian Lu (near Jiangning Lu)

🚇 Shimen Lu/
   Huangpi Nan Lu   ☎ 021-6215-7566

🕐 10:30am–9:00pm

💲 💲   💳 All major credit cards

🇻

This restaurant is not only vegetarian, it also promotes a lifestyle of no meat, no smoking, no egg and no alcohol. Mock meat dishes are prepared lovingly and presented beautifully, with very little oil and no msg. We highly recommend you try this for a simple, light and delicious meal. Meals cost approximately RMB40–80 per person.

Vegetarian Lifestyle

848 Huangjin Cheng Dao (near Shuicheng Nan Lu)

Take a taxi to Hongqiao District

021-6275-1798

10:30am–9:00pm

$ $ All major credit cards

Meals cost approximately RMB40–80 per person.

Vegetarian Lifestyle

77 Songshan Lu (via Huaihai Zhong Lu)

Located in Luwan District

021-5306-8001

10:30am–9:00pm

$ $ All major credit cards

Meals cost approximately RMB40–80 per person.

NON-CHINESE CUISINE

'You've come a long way baby' is what can be said about the development of international cuisine choices in Shanghai over the last ten years. From a time when the only foreign food options were a handful of five-star hotel restaurants and fast food chains, Shanghai can now boast a world-class line up of top restaurants.

The city has become one of the most exciting new places globally for independent and international restaurateurs to make their mark. In doing so, they are creating some of the finest new restaurants in the world for travellers to explore.

Asian

Indian / South Asian

Hazara

🍴 Building 4, Ruijin Guest House,118 Ruijin Er Lu

🧭 Situated between Yongjia Lu and Fuxing Zhong Lu

🚇 Shanxi Nan Lu   ☎ 021-6466-4328

🕐 5:30am–10:30pm (Sun–Thu); 5:30pm–11:00pm (Fri–Sat)

💲 💲 💲 💲   💳 All major credit cards

V

Situated in the Face complex of an old villa in the middle of one of Shanghai's beautiful old estates, Hazara is as graceful and pleasant as its name suggests. The service is excellent and the curries memorable. Meals cost approximately RMB250–300 per person.

Indian Kitchen

🍴 572 Yongjia Lu

🧭 Located between Yueyang Lu and Wulumuqi Nan Lu

🚇 Hengshan Lu   ☎ 021-6473-1517

🕐 11:00am–2:00pm, 5:00pm–11:00pm

💲 💲   💳 All major credit cards

V

A favourite among Shanghai residents, including Indian expats, the food is authentic and the environment fun. At this outlet, you can watch dough twirling through the air. This then becomes the roti that will arrive to your table minutes later. Meals cost approximately RMB80–100 per person.

Indian Kitchen

 House 8, 3911 Hongmei Lu (near Yan An Xi Lu)

Hengshan Lu   021-6261-0377

🕒 11:00am–2:00pm, 5:00pm–11:00pm

💲 💲   All major credit cards

Meals cost approximately RMB80–100 per person.

Indian Kitchen

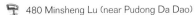 480 Minsheng Lu (near Pudong Da Dao)

Hengshan Lu   021-5821-9875

🕒 11:00am–2:00pm, 5:00pm–11:00pm

💲 💲   All major credit cards

Meals cost approximately RMB80–100 per person.

Indian Kitchen

 600 Lantian Lu, Green Spots and Leisure Centre (near Biyun Lu)

Hengshan Lu   021-5030-2005

🕒 11:00am–2:00pm, 5:00pm–11:00pm

💲 💲   All major credit cards

Meals cost approximately RMB80–100 per person.

Kaveen's Kitchen

2/F, 231 Huashan Lu (near Yan An Xi Lu)

Jing An Temple 021-6248-8292

11:30am–2:30pm, 5:00pm–12:00pm

$ $ $ $ Cash only

V

This restaurant has commanded an extremely loyal following in Shanghai. In part because of the kindness of the owner and his restaurant staff, and in part because of the excellent food. Both are important endorsements and you will often be sitting side by side with Indian families who are regulars. Meals are medium to high priced, depending on how many dishes you order.

Punjabi

N3, No.12-20, Peace Square, 18 Shuicheng Lu

Situated near Hongqiao Lu

021-6278-8626

10:30am–11:30pm

$ $ $ All major credit cards

V

Although the number of dishes is somewhat limited, Punjabi is highly regarded because of its well-priced buffet and free beer. Usually, a group performs Indian folk songs to accompany your dining experience. Meals cost approximately RMB150 per couple.

Punjabi

2/F 102 Xiangyang Lu (near Nanchang Lu)

Shanxi Nan Lu 021-6472-5464 / 021-6472-5465

10:30am–11:30pm

$ $ $ All major credit cards

V

Meals cost approximately RMB150 per couple.

Tandoor

 59 Maoming Nan Lu, South Building, Jin Jiang Hotel (near Changle Lu)

 Shanxi Nan Lu   021-6472-5494

 11:30am–2:00pm, 5:30pm–10:30pm

      All major credit cards

The first classy restaurant to dine in apart from hotels, Tandoori has kept its tradition of offering excellent food in a gorgeous space. Walk through the arches and be transported to a more mystical, exotic place. Meals cost approximately RMB150–200 per person.

Japanese

Ambrosia

 2-3/F, 150 Fengyang Lu (near Yueyang Lu)

 Hengshan Lu   021-6431-3935

 5.30pm–11:00pm (weekdays);
11:00am–2:00pm, 5:30pm–11:00pm (weekends)

      All major credit cards

Housed in a gorgeous old villa, the attention to detail in food, service and ambiance makes this a top choice for special occasions. Meals cost approximately RMB350 per person.

Shintori Null II

 803 Julu Lu (near Fumin Lu)

 Changshu Lu   021-5404-5252

 5:30pm–11:00pm (weekdays);
11:30am–2:00pm, 5:00pm–11:00pm (weekends)

      All major credit cards

Sleek, trendy, unique and very Shanghai, the newest Shintori restaurant is worth a visit just to experience the ambiance. If you have trouble getting a table, it is entertaining to sit at the sushi bar watching skilled chefs with knives and capable hands create beautiful dishes. Meals cost approximately RMB200–250 per person.

Tairyo

139 Ruijin Yi Lu (near Changle Lu)

Shanxi Nan Lu   021-5382-8818

10:30am–2:00pm, 5:00pm–11:00pm

All major credit cards

A chain best known for group nights out, Tairyo offers all you can eat and drink for RMB150. Dining here is all about volume and fun. Buffet dinner costs approximately RMB150 per person.

Tairyo

943 Hongxu Lu (near Yan An Xi Lu)

021-6242-2190

10:30am–2:00pm, 5:00pm–11:00pm

All major credit cards

Buffet dinner costs approximately RMB150 per person.

Tairyo

5/F Westgate Mall Isetan, 1038 Nanjing Xi Lu (near Jiangning Lu)

021-6218-3047

10:30am–2:00pm, 5:00pm–11:00pm

All major credit cards

Buffet dinner costs approximately RMB150 per person.

Tairyo

3/F Hong Kong Plaza, 283 Huai Hai Zhong Lu (near Liulin Lu)

Huangpi Nan Lu   021-6390-7244

10:30am–2:00pm, 5:00pm–11:00pm

$ $ $ All major credit cards

Buffet dinner costs approximately RMB150 per person.

Tairyo

1288 Hongqiao Lu (near Songyuan Lu)

021-6278-3105

10:30am–2:00pm, 5:00pm–11:00pm

$ $ $ All major credit cards

Buffet dinner costs approximately RMB150 per person.

Tokio Joe

2A Gaolan Lu (in Fuxing Park, near Sinan Lu)

Huangpi Nan Lu   021-5383-2328

11:30am–2:30pm, 6:00pm–11:00pm

$ $ $ All major credit cards

True to its name, Tokio Joe is the westernised version of a Japanese eatery. Chunky California rolls and smooth miso soup are west coast comfort food, in a sharp modern environment. Through the restaurant windows, patrons can watch people stroll and chat in Fuxing Park. Meals cost approximately RMB150 per person.

Yin

Jin Jiang Hotel Gourmet Street, 59 Maoming Nan Lu
(near Changle Lu)

Shanxi Nan Lu   021-5466-5070

Noon–2:00pm, 6:00pm–10:00pm

💲💲💲💲💲   All major credit cards

Yin is consistently designated as serving the best Japanese food in Shanghai by aficionados who have spent years in Japan earning the title. The restaurant is located in the grounds of the Jin Jiang Hotel, next to the building that Nixon stayed in when he visited China to sign the famous Shanghai Accord. Yin is priced between medium and high range, depending on how many dishes you order.

Korean

Arirang

28 Jiangsu Bei Lu (near Changning Lu)

Jiangsu Lu   021-6252-7146

10:30am–10:30pm

💲💲💲   All major credit cards

Best known for its meat dishes that are cooked on hot coals in front of diners, Arirang is one of Shanghai's oldest Korean eateries. It is priced medium to high range, depending on how many dishes you order.

Gaoli

No.1, Lane 181, Wuyuan Lu (Wulumuqi Zhong Lu)

Changshu Lu   021-6431-5236

10:00am–2:00am

💲   All major credit cards

Situated at the rear of one of Shanghai's famous old guesthouses, the location of Donghu makes it an excellent choice for a weekend afternoon meal. Excellent kimchi and meats which patrons cook themselves make it an interactive dining experience. Meals cost approximately RMB50 per person.

Gaoli

 1/F Donghu Guest House, 7 Donghu Lu (near Huaihai Zhong Lu)

 Shanxi Nan Lu   021-6415-8158 / 7400

 10:00am–2:00am

           All major credit cards

Meals cost approximately RMB50 per person.

Korean BBQ

 3/F Hongqiao New Town Club, 35 Loushan Guan Lu (near Yan An Xi Lu)

 Situated in Changning District

 021-6270-6317

 11:30am–10:00pm

  All major credit cards

This restaurant is popular because it uses extremely fresh ingredients. Add the meats and vegetables to the dish by yourself. After you have finished your meal, a soup, flavoured by the meats and vegetables, will be left in the bowl for you to drink. Buffet meal costs approximately RMB158 per person.

Southeast Asian

Bali Laguna

189 Huashan Lu

Situated inside Jing An Park

Jing An Temple   021-6248-6970

11:00am–2:30pm, 6:00pm–10:30pm

 All major credit cards

Bali Laguna, in the middle of Jing An Park, offers patrons the choice of dining beside a small lake, or in the restaurant's basement which is partially submerged, with the water from the lake at eye level. There are a number of tasty speciality dishes served here so ask the restaurant staff for recommendations. Meals cost approximately RMB150–200 per person.

Frankie's Place

546 Huanghua Lu (near Hongjing Lu)

Situated in Minhang District

021-5476-1068

9:30am–11:00pm

All major credit cards

A favourite among Singaporean and Malaysian expats, Frankie's Place has a solid track record in Shanghai. The food is as spicy as the decoration is plain. Pricing here is medium range, depending on how many dishes you order.

Thai

Banana Leaf

 4/F Hong Kong Plaza South Tower, 283 Huaihai Zhong Lu
(near Huangpi Nan Lu)

 Huangpi Nan Lu   📞 021-5383-3333

🕐 11:00am–11:00pm

💲 💲 💲 💲   💳 All major credit cards

🌱

A spacious, lively bustling restaurant, the Banana Leaf is popular among
Shanghainese. It serves medium to high range food, depending on how
many dishes you order.

Coconut Paradise

 38 Fuming Lu (near Julu Lu)

 Jing An Temple   📞 021-6248-1998

🕐 11:00am–2:00pm, 5:00pm–11:00pm

💲 💲 💲 💲   💳 All major credit cards

🌱

Situated in an old villa, Coconut Paradise offers authentic Thai food as
the chef and owners have retained the regional tastes and dishes of
Chiang Mai. A good wine selection is available. Meals cost approximately
RMB200–300 per person.

Irene's Thai

 263 Tongren Lu (between Nanjing Xi Lu and Beijing Xi Lu)

✛ Located in Jing An District, take a taxi from Jing An Temple
metro station

 Jing An Temple   📞 021-6247-3579

🕐 11:00am–2:00pm, 6:00pm–10:00pm

💲 💲 💲   💳 All major credit cards

🌱

Set in an old villa, Irene's boasts great ambiance and authentic Thai
cuisine. Meals cost approximately RMB150–200 per person.

Lan Na Thai

Building 4, Ruijin Guest House, 118 Ruijin Er Lu

Located in Luwan District, between Yongjia Lu and Fuxing Zhong Lu

Shanxi Nan Lu   021-6466-4328

Noon–2:30pm, 5:30pm–10:30pm (Sun–Thu)
Noon–2:30pm, 5:30pm–11:00pm (Fri–Sat)

$ $ $ $ All major credit cards

V

Located within the Face compound, Lan Na Thai is popular among people entertaining guests from out of town. Beautiful private rooms make the perfect setting for small groups. Meals cost approximately RMB250–300 per person.

Simply Thai

5C Dongping Lu (between Hengshan Lu and Yueyang Lu)

Hengshan Lu   021-6445-9551

11:00am–11:00pm

$ $ $ All major credit cards

V

Meals cost approximately RMB100 per person.

Simply Thai

No 27, Lane 181 Taicang Lu (corner of Madang Lu and Xingye Lu)

Huangpi Nan Lu   021-6326-2088

11:00am–Midnight

$ $ $ All major credit cards

V

Meals cost approximately RMB100 per person.

Vietnamese

Cochinchina

Building 11, 889 Julu Lu (near Changshu Lu)

Changshu Lu   021-6445-6797

11:00am–11:00pm

💲💲💲   All major credit cards

One of the first Asian restaurants to capture the charm of old Shanghai, Cochinchina is located in an old villa, giving it the elegance of French-inspired, old Vietnam. Depending on how many dishes you order, an average meal can cost approximately RMB150 per person.

Fong's

2/F Lippo Plaza, 222 Huaihai Zhong Lu
(near Songshan Lu)

Huangpi Nan Lu   021-6387-7228

11:00am–10:30pm

💲💲💲💲   All major credit cards

The menu is standard Vietnamese fare with a touch of influence from China. Fong's is priced medium to high range, depending on how many dishes you order.

Pho

📠 781 Huangjin Cheng Dao (near Gubei Lu)

🧭 Located in Hongkou District

📞 021-6209-7669

🕙 9:30am–Midnight

💲 💲 💲 💲

🧾 All major credit cards

Situated in one of the old commercial districts of Shanghai, Pho brings Vietnamese flavours to the heart of Shanghai. Pho, pronounced *fuh,* is a traditional Vietnamese soup made with rice noodles. It comes in a clear broth and contains thin cuts of meat, seasoned with vegetables, herbs, lime and chillis. Pho restaurant is priced medium to high range, depending on how many dishes you order.

Temple Saigon

📠 1731 Huashan Lu (near Huaihai Xi Lu)

🚡 Xujiahui

📞 021-6281-8427 /
021-6281-8428

🕙 11:00am–11:30pm

💲 💲 💲

🧾 All major credit cards

Located in the heart of the old French Concession, the restaurant does a great job of creating an atmosphere which is slower than the usual bustle of Shanghai. Seafood dishes are fresh and well-prepared. Vietnamese coffee is an excellent way to finish the meal. Meals cost approximately RMB150–200 per person.

Non-Asian

American

Blue Frog

207 Maoming Nan Lu (near Fuxing Lu)

021-6445-6634

10:00am–2:00am

All major credit cards

This restaurant chain was the first to put fun in food, adult style. With its 'Martinis and Manicures' nights, this branch is a favourite with the lunch and after work crowd. Meals cost approximately RMB50–70 per person.

Blue Frog

86 Tongren Lu (near Nanjing Xi Lu)

Situated in Jing An District

Jing An Temple   021-6247-0320

10:00am–2:00am

All major credit cards

This branch is a favourite with the lunch and after work crowd. Meals cost approximately RMB50–70 per person.

Blue Frog

Green Sports & Leisure Centre, R3-633 Biyun Lu

Located in Pudong District

021-5030-6426

10:00am–2:00am

All major credit cards

This outlet is better suited to families. Meals cost approximately RMB50–70 per person.

Blue Frog

Lane 3338, House 30, Hongmei Lu

Located in Hongqiao District

021-5422-5119

10:00am–2:00am

All major credit cards

This outlet is better suited to families. It even boasts a sweets bar for children that exactly mimics the chocolate factory from the bestseller *Charlie and the Chocolate Factory*. Meals cost approximately RMB50–70 per person.

Element Fresh

Room 112, Shanghai Centre, 1376 Nanjing Xi Lu (near Xikang Lu)

Situated in Jing An District

Jing An Temple   021-6279-8682

7:00am–11:00pm

All major credit cards

A Shanghai expat favourite, Element Fresh make addictive smoothies and the best salads in Shanghai. They also make the best soy milk coffee latte in town. The staffing at the restaurants is consistent, providing some of the best service in Shanghai. The place is always buzzing. Meals cost approximately RMB50–100 per person.

Malone's

255 Tongren Lu (near Nanjing Xi Lu)

Situated in Jing An District

Jing An Temple   021-6247-2400

11:00am–2:00am

💲💲   All major credit cards

V

The original best burger in Shanghai, Malone's is an institution. Opened more than 10 years ago, it has a pack of faithful followers who are there for lunch, after work drinks and dinner. The menu features all-things American, from mexican dishes to pizza. Savvy to cross-cultural dining, Malone's also has a selection of Asian dishes to cater to less adventurous Chinese guests. Meals cost approximately RMB50–100 per person.

Moon River Diner

No 17, Lane 3338 Hongmei Lu (near Yan An Xi Lu)

Located in Hongqiao District

021-6465-8879

8:00am–10:00pm

💲💲   Cash only

V

Once you have had Moon River hashbrowns for breakfast you will keep coming back, just like the rest of us. Some people also place delivery orders solely for milkshakes, which are highly addictive. From the jukebox to the neon lights, Moon River is as close as you can get to a real diner this side of the Pacific. It has wireless computer access for those who can not be too far from email at any time. Meals cost approximately RMB50–100 per person.

European

Cafe Montmartre (French)

 55-57 Xiangyang Nan Lu (near Huahai Zhong Lu)

Changshu Lu ☎ 021-5404-6777

🕐 9:00am–Midnight

💲 💲 💲 All major credit cards

This is a great place to settle for a meal after a stint of tough bargaining at the notorious Xiangyang 'fakes' Market. Cafe Montmartre is set in an old building at the edge of the market. Its covered terrace seating is eye level with the trees that border the market area. Meals cost approximately RMB100–200 per person.

Casanova (Italian)

Building 3-4, 913 Julu Lu (near Changshu Lu)

☎ 021-5403-4528

🕐 11:30am–11:00pm

💲 💲 💲 💲 💲 All major credit cards

Situated in a roomy old villa in the French Concession, Casanova is a great place for a lingering evening meal. A signature restaurant in which to host guests from outside Shanghai, the food is tasty and the wine list is comprehensive. Meals cost approximately RMB300+ per person.

Da Marco (Italian)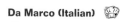

🍴 103 Dongzhuanbang Lu (near Zhenning Lu)

📞 021-6210-4495

🕐 Noon–11:00pm

💲 💲 💲

💳 All major credit cards

🗸

This is the Italian restaurant in Shanghai that the Italians love to go to. Da Marco has a loyal following based upon the quality of its food and the feeling you get in the dining room that you are settling in for a good night in an Italian village. It is a place for friends, food and chat. Best to book in advance. Meals cost approximately RMB100–200 per person.

Da Marco (Italian)

🍴 62 Yandang Lu (near Huaihai Zhong Lu)

📞 021-6385-5998

🕐 Noon–11:00pm

💲 💲 💲

💳 All major credit cards

🗸

Meals cost approximately RMB100–200 per person.

Dan's Old Farmhouse (German)

🍴 318 Julu Lu (near Maoming Nan Lu)

📞 021-6258-5560

🕐 5:00pm–Midnight (weekdays);
11:00am–Midnight (weekends)

💲 💲 💲

💳 All major credit cards

🗸

Dan's background as a butcher comes through in the great cuts of meat that are available at the restaurant. He supplies many of Shanghai's top restaurants with their sausage and meat cuts and for authentic German fare, Dan's is an excellent choice. Meals cost approximately RMB100–200 per person.

Jean Georges (French)

 3 Zhongshan Dong Yi Lu (near Guangdong Lu)

 021-6321-7733

 11:30am–10:00pm

  All major credit cards

Part of the Three on the Bund group, it is hard to decide whether lunch or dinner is better at this restaurant. One of the best kept secrets in Shanghai, Jean Georges' set lunch menu is a delight and well worth getting in trouble with your boss over a late return to your office. At night, the view of Pudong is stunning. Meals cost approximately RMB300+ per person.

Le Bouchon (French)

 1455 Wuding Xi Lu (near Jiangsu Lu)

 021-6255-7088

 6:30pm–11:00pm

  All major credit cards

Having the best ambiance in the city, Le Bouchon is one of the few restaurants where you can hear the rain on the roof on a stormy Shanghai night. Designed to embrace the ancient tree that cuts through the dining room, each visit to the restaurant is made a treat thanks to the owners. The menu has variety and the ever changing specials board will be read to you if French is not your first language. Favourite dishes are the rich scallop tart and hearty steaks. Book in advance as it is always full. Meals cost approximately RMB300+ per person.

Paulaner Brauhaus (German)

150 Fenyang Lu (near Yueyang Lu)

021-6474-5700

5:00pm–2:00am

💲 💲 💲 💲

All major credit cards

This is the first German restaurant chain in Shanghai. The Paulaner group has brought the noisy, festive feeling of a Munich beer hall to some very scenic parts of Shanghai. It offers sampler plates that allow you to taste different German sausages. Accompany this with home brewed beer and a lively Filipino band. Meals cost approximately RMB200–300 per person.

Paulaner Brauhaus (German)

House 19-20, North Block Xintiandi, Lane 181 Taicang Lu

021-6320-3935

5:00pm–2:00am

💲 💲 💲 💲

All major credit cards

Meals cost approximately RMB200–300 per person.

Paulaner Brauhaus (German)

Binjiang Da Dao, Fudu Duan (next to Pudong Shangrila Hotel)

021-6888-3935

5:00pm–2:00am

💲 💲 💲 💲

All major credit cards

Meals cost approximately RMB200–300 per person.

Sandoz (Portuguese)

 B8-207 Maoming Lu (near Yongjia Lu)

 021-6466-0479

 11:30am–10:00pm

$ $ $ All major credit cards

V

Nestled near the end of Maoming Lu, on the edge of one of Shanghai's oldest guesthouses, Sandoz offers a tasty selction of Portuguese food. The seating is ideal for small groups. It is a great place at the weekend as one can easily move from the restaurant to the live music playing at the House of Blues and Jazz nearby, or go bar hopping down Maoming Lu. Meals cost approximately RMB100–200 per person.

International mix

239

 239 Shimenyi Lu (near Weihai Lu)

 Located in Jing An District

Shimen Lu   021-6253-2837

11:00am–8:00pm

                              All major credit cards

The great food that you will have is worth the effort to find 239, one of Shanghai's newest and slickest restaurants. Its subtly branded, trendy black sliding doors are camped under a large 'Office Superstore' sign. A stream of socialites come through the doors, from professional business people to professional models. Dishes to try are the seared tuna which melts in your mouth, and most other dishes complement it well. Meals cost approximately RMB200–300 per person.

Azul

18 Dongping Lu (near Wulumuqi Lu)

                              021-6433-1172

11:00am–1:00am

                              All major credit cards

Founded by Peruvian chef Eduardo, who has opened a string of successful Shanghai hotspots, Azul makes it difficult to pick a favourite dish. Almost anything you choose from the menu will be a treat. Eduardo has drawn on his Peruvian heritage and global culinary experiences to create such a mouth-watering menu of unique food. The environment is also fashionably festive. Meals cost approximately RMB200–300 per person.

M on the Bund

🍴 7th Floor, 20 Guandong Lu (near Zhongshan Dong Yi Lu)

☎ 021-6350-9988

🕐 11:30am–10:30pm

💲 💲 💲 💲 💲

💳 All major credit cards

🍷

No view is better, no service more attentive and no menu more Shanghai. M on the Bund has been on the must go list for celebrities and superstars since it first opened. It equally attracts the local community as there is nothing as wonderful as sitting out on the restaurant balcony sipping wine while the lights go out on the Bund. The management of this establishment have made it a special place to dine, both through their attention to creating a perfect dining experience and through their open-hearted contribution to the community. It is a Shanghai icon. Book in advance. Meals cost approximately RMB300+ per person.

Mesa

🍴 748 Julu Lu (near Fumin Lu)

☎ 021-6289-9108

🕐 6:00pm–11:30pm

💲 💲 💲 💲

💳 All major credit cards

🍷

When two top Shanghai restaurant veterans got together, Mesa was the result. It is a place that perfectly balances slick, trendy design with a comfortable, relaxing atmosphere. The menu is one that you will want to work your way through visit after visit. Mesa is another of Shanghai's evening hotspots, so it is best to book in advance. Meals cost approximately RMB200–300 per person.

For special
occasions

Breakfast

In Shanghai, breakfast is a sociable event. During the week, it is an opportunity to get a head start on networking and business deals for the day. At weekends, families and friends take the time to leisurely catch-up. The restaurants included in this section are selected not just for food quality, but also for their networking quality.

Element Fresh

Room 112, Shanghai Centre, 1376 Nanjing Xi Lu (near Xikang Lu)

Located in Jing An District

Jing An Temple   021-6279-8682

7:00am–11:00pm

All major credit cards

At the weekend, sunny mornings find people vying for an outdoor seat. During the week, the professional crowd wave at each other over copies of the Financial Times. Element Fresh has great American breakfast sets and fresh juices. Meals cost approximately RMB50–100 per person.

Moon River Diner

No 17, Lane 3338 Hongmei Lu (near Yan An Xi Lu)

Located in Hongqiao District

021-6465-8879

8:00am–10:00pm

All major credit cards

At Moon River Diner, it is the hashbrowns that have people lined up outside the door at weekends, sipping bottomless cups of coffee and chatting as they wait for a table to become available. This establishment is popular with children as there are free balloons and a playground across from the front door on the pedestrian walkway. Meals cost approximately RMB50–100 per person.

Moon River Diner

🚇 Thumb Plaza, 2nd Floor, Unit 38, 199 Fangdian Lu
(near Dingxiang Lu)

🎯 Situated in Pudong District

🚇 Science & Technology Museum 　　📞 021-5033-5900

🕐 8:00am–10:00pm

💲 💲 　　　　　　　　　　💳 All major credit cards

🍴

Meals cost approximately RMB50–100 per person.

Vienna Cafe

🚇 House 2, 25 Shaoxing Lu (near Shanxi Nan Lu)

📞 021-6445-2131

🕐 8:00am–8:00pm

💲 💲 　　　　　　　　　　💳 Cash only

🍴

Vienna Cafe is a step back in time. Its high ceilings and smell of coffee and freshly baked pastries have you settling in for a leisurely morning. Skim the newspaper, write in a journal or update friends on the adventures of the previous day. The owner/Viennese baker will personally take your order. Meals cost approximately RMB50–100 per person.

Wagas 🍴

🚇 In the basement next to McDonalds, CITIC Square, 1168 Nanjing Xi Lu (near Shanxi Bei Lu)

🎯 Located in Jing An District

🚇 Jing An Temple 　　📞 021-5292-5228

🕐 10:00am–2:00am

💲 💲 💲 　　　　　　　　💳 All major credit cards

🍴

The service is fast, the seating comfortable and the people watching excellent. Wagas is great for a leisurely breakfast. Depending on your state from the night before, either the hangover sandwich or the corn cakes are an excellent choice. The caffe lattes are some of the best in Shanghai. Meals cost approximately RMB100–200 per person.

Outdoor

From spring to autumn, Shanghai residents can be found enjoying lunches and evening meals under graceful old trees in the French Concession area and on Bund-view terraces along the Huangpu River. Eating outdoors is one of the most enjoyable ways to capture the spirit of old Shanghai.

Kabb

 Unit 1, House 5, North Block Xintiandi, Lane 181 Taicang Lu (near Madang Lu)

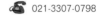 021-3307-0798

🕐 10:00am–11:00pm

 All major credit cards

One of the first restaurants to open in Xintiandi, Kabb is a favourite outdoor location for business lunchers, afternoon lingerers and the after work crowd. The food is a modern American style, although there are plenty of standard comfort food dishes to give you that taste of home you may be missing. Meals cost approximately RMB100–200 per person.

Kathleen's 5

5th Floor, Shanghai Art Museum, 325 Nanjing Xi Lu (near Huangpi Nan Lu)

People's Park   021-6327-2221

🕐 11:30am–Midnight

All major credit cards

Some of the most interesting modern architecture in Shanghai is your backdrop when eating a meal on the terrace at Kathleen's 5. K5 is on the roof of the vintage Shanghai Art Museum that borders People's Park and has a view of the iconic Shanghai Opera House and Shanghai Museum. The backdrop is the Pudong skyline and the food is continental. Meals cost approximately RMB200–300 per person.

O'Malley's

 42 Taojiang Lu (near Wulumuqi Nan Lu)

 021-6474-6166

🕐 11:00am–1:00am

💲 💲 💲   All major credit cards

V

From big screen televisions broadcasting football or rugby from distant shores to the more immediate noise of children in full battle in the colourful playground, the walled garden of O'Malley's is one of the better outdoor spots in which to eat. The food is standard Irish pub fare. Meals cost approximately RMB100–200 per person.

Sasha's

 House 11, No 19 Dongping Lu (near Hengshan Lu)

 021-6474-6166

🕐 11:30am–2:00am

💲 💲 💲 💲   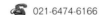 All major credit cards

V

The courtyard of choice for Shanghai veterans, nestled in the heart of the old French Concession, Sasha's is occupied late into the evening with tables full of leisurely diners. On a clear night, the moon can be seen rising over the roof of an old villa that was the home to two of the famous Soong sisters, whose husbands were General Chiang Kai-shek and financial wizard HH Kung. The food at Sasha's is continental and the chef is European. Meals cost approximately RMB200–300 per person.

Romance

There is a good reason why Shanghai has been known for generations as the 'Paris of the East' — it is a very romantic city. Finding your own private space away from the crowd is something of an art form. Committed to supporting your romantic pursuits, the authors' favourites are listed below.

M on the Bund

🖐 7th Floor, 20 Guandong Lu (near Zhongshan Dong Yi Lu)

✛ Found in a cosy corner of the Glamour Room

📞 021-6350-9988

🕐 11:30am–10:30pm

💲💲💲💲💲   💳 All major credit cards

Ⅴ

By night, the restaurant is candle-lit, the beaded fixtures and dark windows shimmering. Add further sparkle with a glass of champagne. It comes with all the personal touches that M on the Bund is known for, from food to finish. Meals cost approximately RMB300+ per person.

New Heights

🖐 7th Floor, Three on the Bund, 3 Zhongshan Dong Yi Lu (near Guangdong Lu)

✛ Situated in the private room of the restaurant, in the turret on the rooftop

📞 021-6321-0909

🕐 11:30am–11:30pm

💲💲💲💲💲   💳 All major credit cards

Ⅴ

How much more romantic could Shanghai be than when viewed from a private skyline turret on the Bund? Call in advance to arrange your own secluded getaway in one of the two private rooms in the turret situated in the corner of the building. Enjoy the fusion cuisine of this Three on the Bund signature restaurant. You will be sure to take home a treasured memory. It does not really matter if you only want to go at night for the romantic *juju*. Meals cost approximately RMB300+ per person.

The Door

🖐 4th Floor, 1468 Hongqiao Lu (near Yan An Xi Lu)

🚆 Hongqiao Lu   📞 021-6295-3737

🕐 6:00pm–2:00am

💲💲💲💲💲   💳 All major credit cards

Ⅴ

The Door is watched over by a giant carved buddha that sits above the entrance. After a beautifully presented, elegant meal, you can sit in soft light and listen to Chinese musicians fuse the haunting sounds of their ancient instruments with new melodies. The improvisation that sometimes occurs resembles a top jazz club. Meals cost approximately RMB300+ per person.

TMSK

 Unit 2, House 11, North Block Xintiandi, Lane 181 Taicang Lu (near Madang Lu)

 021-6326-2227

 1:30pm–12:30am

       All major credit cards

Conceived by celebrity artists, TMSK is also an abbreviation for the *pinying* expression meaning 'transparent thinking'. Every item designed in this restaurant takes its cue from beautiful coloured handspun translucent glass, to eating utensils to staircase fixtures. With plenty of mood lighting, accented by shimmering metal screens, wire mesh lanterns, textured mirrors and plenty of carved tiles and wood features, TMSK is the perfect backdrop for a memorable night. Well presented food and excellent service make this restaurant the perfect place for a romatic evening.

Whampoa Club

 No 3, The Bund, 5th Floor, 3 Zhongshan Dong Yi Lu

 Situated near Guangdong Lu

 021-6321-3737

11:30am–2:30pm, 5:30pm–10:00pm

      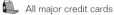 All major credit cards

Whampoa Club offers Shanghainese dining at a new level of taste, style and presentation. The founding chef, Jereme Leung, is one of Asia's youngest master chefs. The club has six private dining rooms and three private tearooms.

Index by restaurant name

Index by district

Index by metro station

Index by local food item

About
the authors

Marybelle Hu

Born in Taiwan, although she has lived within numerous cultures, Marybelle Hu remains close to her Chinese heritage in many ways. This is evident through her typically Chinese respect and passion for food. As a resident of Shanghai for the past twelve years, Marybelle has an almost local knowledge of the city's food. Marybelle is the co-owner of Hu & Hu, one of Shanghai's most successful Chinese antique furniture shops and along with several partners, has recently opened an American style diner.

Angie Eagan

Typical of many long-term Shanghai residents, Angie Eagan came to the city on a two week business trip and eleven years later is still exploring the alleys and parks of Shanghai. Angie is the Vice President of China for Young & Rubicam Brands, one of the world's top communications agencies. When not supporting the world's top companies in building their China brands, she spends her time exploring and mapping the ever-changing Shanghai scene. She is a past-Chairman of the American Chamber of Commerce in Shanghai and a founder of nonprofit Mongolia Sunrise to Sunset.

Justina Tulloch

Coming from a well known Australian wine family, Justina Tulloch developed a passion for good food and wine from an early age. Following a career in professional services marketing in both Australia and China, Justina decided to follow her calling and undertook a commercial cookery course in Australia in 2002. Justina has been a resident of Shanghai for over seven years and has experienced the best and worst of Shanghai dining during that time. She is currently experiencing a whole new challenge, dining out in Shanghai with her two boys under the age of two.